# BORN

— TO BE —

# RICH

# BORN

### — TO BE —

# RICH

ROLLAN A. ROBERTS II

Tate Publishing & *Enterprises*

Published by Tate Publishing & Enterprises, LLC
127 E. Trade Center Terrace | Mustang, Oklahoma 73064 USA
1.888.361.9473 | www.tatepublishing.com

Tate Publishing is committed to excellence in the publishing industry. The company reflects the philosophy established by the founders, based on Psalms 68:11,
*"The Lord gave the word and great was the company of those who published it."*

Book design copyright © 2007 by Tate Publishing, LLC. All rights reserved.
*Cover design by Taylor Rauschkolb*
*Interior design by Lynly D. Taylor*

Published in the United States of America
ISBN: 978-1-60247-371-3

07.05.11

*This book is dedicated to my wife and parents who have supported me in all the risks that I have taken to achieve my dreams. They stood with me when others would not. Thank you for your love and support!*

# TABLE OF CONTENTS

# FOREWORD

Whether you have hundreds of books on how to build wealth, or this is the first in your collection, *Born to be Rich* provides an excellent road map filled with life changing principles. In this book, Rollan talks not only about pure wealth building, but also how to develop and prosper in other aspects of life by providing you with very clear principles and direction on how to become successful in each area. If you picked up this book only expecting to learn how to build wealth, you are about to receive more than you bargained for.

This book is as much an autobiography as it is a knowledge tool. This is a story of his successes and failures, and the valuable lessons he has learned along the way. I have personally known Rollan for several years, and can attest to the fact that he lives what he teaches. Rarely have I had the opportunity to meet an individual that so deeply believes in what he teaches and consistently shows it through his daily actions.

The teachings in this book are priceless. Rollan has taken the time to compile the lessons and principles that have taken him countless hours and thousands of dollars to acquire and has presented them to you in this concise and usable format.

Each chapter is saturated with principles and techniques that have been proven in his own life, and are presented in language that is easy to read and follow. And just in case you missed a principle, each chapter ends with "Reflections on the Riches from this Chapter" to ensure that you know what to focus on. Rollan also does an excellent job of providing real life examples and application to each principle, teaching how to recognize success and avoid failure.

I highly recommend *Born to be Rich* to those individuals that have a true interest in building riches, gaining power and knowledge, developing successful relationships, and are committed to controlling their circumstances; or as Rollan calls them, "the 5%'ers". Once you truly believe and act upon the principles you learn in this book you will be amazed at what you have the power to accomplish regardless of your current circumstances or position.

### KYLE JOHNSON

*Vice President and General Manager, Indirect Sales*

# INTRODUCTION

What were you born for? Do you know? What is your purpose on earth? What are you destined for? Are riches and wealth beyond imagination your destiny? They can be. They are attracted into your life by the way you think and act toward them. The following pages will make you more money than you will ever know what to do with. They will take you to a level of success that you have only longed for. If you are already a success, you will appreciate the lessons that you learned along the way and perhaps didn't even realize that you learned them. You will be encouraged and inspired to continue your journey of success and will be stirred to reach even greater heights.

I know what I was born for. I was born to make a difference in the lives of others, and a life filled with riches and wealth can be of great assistance in that endeavor. I was born into a very poor family. My parents eventually ended up in the middle class range living paycheck to paycheck (They are doing great today. I owe them everything I am, own, and hope to be for their constant encouragement, support, and work ethic they instilled in me.). I grew up in West Virginia. They have the highest percentage of obese people in the nation, and they have the highest percentage of people per capita on welfare. They have learned how to repel riches and wealth in their life. They have learned exactly what not to do. Their contentment to stay this way was perhaps one of the greatest sources of irritation for me. I wanted to do more, be more, and accomplish more. It should have come as no surprise that people didn't think it could be done. It is not a coincidence that people told me that I was too big a dreamer; that it would never happen for me. I am appalled by the financial ignorance that willingly prevails in our society. The majority of people don't have the desire to learn how to be rich. They think that it is a matter of luck or of winning the lottery. It is neither of these things, but they refuse to educate themselves as to what makes the financial world tick, even though it extends its long arm into their daily lives and directly determines where they live, what size house they have, what and how many cars they have, what kind, if any, vacations are taken, and how many groceries can be bought. Yet, this is not a strong enough motivator to move them to educate themselves voluntarily on monetary issues.

But you and I were born to be rich, and we know it. We know where we are destined to go. We know what financial means we are to acquire. We know what kind of wealth we are to manage successfully. We know what levels of greatness we are to attain, and we will voluntarily submit ourselves to the necessary planning and education to accomplish our purpose and mission. We are the few. We are the minority. We are the fearless, and we will not fail. Join me as I walk you through the keys to success and the keys to failure and how to capitalize on the one while avoiding the other. Thank you for reading this book. I wish you all the riches, wealth, and success that you were born to have.

*Chapter 1*

# FAILURE IS EXPENSIVE

The master of the house was going away on a long journey. He would be gone for quite some time. He had three servants to whom he entrusted some of his money to see what they could do with it while he was gone. He gave one servant $1,000. He gave another servant $2,000, and he gave the third servant $5,000. Upon his return, the master of the house asked the three servants what their investments had yielded the master. The servant with $5,000 presented the master with $10,000. The servant with $2,000 gave the master $4,000. The servant with $1,000 said that he put the money in a very safe place so it would not be stolen, and he presented the master with the same $1,000. The master said that he had been slothful and not a good steward of what had been entrusted to his care. The master said to the servants who had generated a profit, "Well done. You've been faithful over a little, now I'll make you ruler over much!"

It was this simple story that I learned while a young child that made me set out on my quest to learn how to be faithful in the little things so that I could be a ruler over much. My parents taught me this lesson from the Bible, and in so doing, gave me the best wealth advice they could have ever given. This book is not for the average person. This book is not even for the above average person. This book is for the person that puts their success and the accomplishment of their goals and dreams on the line, and they will achieve them no matter the cost. They are willing to change, to get better, and to be better. If you ask a room full of people anywhere, even a jail, "Who in here wants to be successful?" most everyone would raise their hand. If everybody everywhere wants to be successful, then why aren't more people successful? What holds them back? If it's true, and it is, that we can have what we dream, be who we want, and do the impossible, then what is the difference between those who do and those who don't? And what about those who are continually persistent, but never seem to achieve what they set out to accomplish? Were they successful? Even if they were, is that the kind of success you want? Success is such an elusive thought. And it is exactly that, a thought. Thought is the only tangible thing from which we create. Nothing is made unless it was first a thought. The most architecturally-amazing buildings, scientific breakthroughs, and significant achievements have come about by thought. We are going to look at some of the ingredients that will determine your level of success. Notice I said "your level" of success. Success is a matter of opinion and means different things to different people. I had people say that I was successful when I didn't feel successful. I'm sure you have felt the same way. One of the reasons this happens is because you are where others want to be, not where you want to be. So to them, you are successful. You have a higher standard for yourself. That is a good thing. It is encouraging to me when someone thinks I'm successful, but I don't feel like I have achieved the level of success that I desire nor am capable of achieving. That's a good feeling to keep. I would be worried if I ever lose that feeling because that feeling is what gets me out of bed in the morning. That feeling is what makes me feel alive. That feeling is what gives me the energy and the enthusiasm to build my business, bring people together, and make my dreams happen. That feeling is a people magnet. People will say that you are driven. They will say you are an over-achiever. You will be called an over-achiever if you are anything above average. Besides, if someone calls me an over-achiever, that simply means that I've achieved more than them! You have to ask, "Compared to what?" Compared to Bill Gates, I'm an under-achiever. Compared to the bum on the street, I'm an over-achiever. And then there is average, somewhere in between these two extremes.

Average, in my opinion, means having good family. It is a $40,000 a year, 8–5 job with a couple weeks vacation, company-paid health insurance, two cars in the garage (with payments on both), a $150,000 house, a little bit of money in a savings account, a mutual fund, credit card debt, and weekend barbeques. That is the picture of average to me. 95% of people will live this way regardless of who writes what, and that is fine. They are entitled to live the life they are comfortable with. Truth is, they probably would not be comfortable living in a mansion and having a fabulous lifestyle because that is not where they are mentally and would either be miserable or lose it all. Look at the majority of lottery winners or any recipient of a large sum of money, including inheritance. Oftentimes, it is quickly squandered away.

However, when I fly over any given town, I see so many housing developments that are built for the "average" person. The majority of houses in any given town seem to be less than 2,500 square feet. They have three bedrooms, two bathrooms, and a two-car garage. And those developments pack you in like rats! Oh, it is an organized rat cage, but from the sky, one person has not achieved more than the next person. In fact, as different as they want to be from each other, they have many more similarities than differences. Then you fly over the house that is away from the hustle and bustle of the town's hub, and you find a beautiful spread. The most luxurious home with a beautifully-shaped, custom-designed pool with an in-ground hot tub with a waterfall and hundred foot water slide that flows into the pool, a three hole golf course in the backyard, a playground twice the size of those in fast food restaurant play-lands, a beautiful circular drive out front with a super-stretch black limousine, a couple of Hummers, a hard top convertible viper, a Bentley... or two, and a various array of exotic automobiles. Then you look off to the side of your palace, and there's the water where you dock your 100' yacht. You look beyond your personal golf course and you see your leer jet that your staff pulled out of the hanger to wash on this beautiful day. Your helipad is right next to your hanger and runway, and you admire your "local transportation." You decide to go back inside the house and shoot some hoops in your full-size, indoor basketball court before heading to the media room to read and meditate and find out what's happening in the world.

My point—that's above average to me. And above average sounds much better to me than average. No matter what you read or whom you listen to, they will all tell you that you have to know exactly what it is you want. You have to become crystal clear. We all know that being crystal clear about what you want isn't enough to get it. There are a lot of people who can tell you exactly what they want, and it's the same thing they wanted 40 years ago. But that is certainly where you start. It could be so much better than the scenario I just described; that's for you to write. I just wanted you to see the difference in living color. Of course, you already knew this. That's why you're reading this book.

I encourage you to eat the meat and spit out the bones as you read through this book. If there is something I say that you don't like, ignore it. If there's something that you like, then use it. There doesn't need to be two Rollans out there. Nobody is going to agree with anybody 100%, and if they do, then one of them isn't necessary. I had to scrape, claw, scrimp, gum, and gnaw my way to where I am today. I didn't catch any breaks; I didn't have a rich uncle that died. I wasn't born with a silver spoon in my mouth or come from a wealthy family. I had to pay my own way through college and graduate school. Nothing has come easy for me. But whoever said that it was supposed to come easy for you? Quit whining, and pay the price. It's not supposed to be easy or everyone would be doing it. I don't want everybody doing it because then I wouldn't be so special! I can't stand it when I hear people make excuses for why they aren't farther along in life than what they are. They blame everyone and everything. "Well, if this didn't happen to me," or "If things went my way, then…" No you wouldn't. You'd still be right where you are because you think like a victim. What you're saying is that you are a product of your environment, and that's not true. You are saying that circumstances make the man, and the truth is that man creates his own circumstances. You choose to be who you are. I don't care where you came from, where you were born, what side of the tracks you grew up on, what schools you went to, who your parents are, or what kind of drugs, alcohol, and gunshots you were around. That should have motivated you to get out of it, not give you an excuse to stay in it. I believe that people find what they are looking for. If you are looking for an excuse disguised as a reason for the way you are, then you will find one. But if you are looking for a reason to be better, then you will certainly find one by looking at the situation you are in and the people you are around. That's why one shoe salesman that got sent to Africa said, "I'm coming home. Nobody over here wears shoes. I can't sell anything over here." The next shoe salesman the company sent to Africa wrote back, "Send another ship loaded with shoes. Nobody over here wears shoes!" Oh yes, you will find what you are looking for. Success doesn't just happen. It is planned. You ask one guy why his life is in the gutter and is going nowhere, and he'll tell you about his poor environment and the greedy rich people that are taking all of his money. Then you ask Oprah Winfrey why her life is a huge monetary success, and she'll tell you that her upbringing and childhood motivated her to be something more because she didn't want to stay there her whole life. Is the difference genetic? Is it a certain personality? That's what a loser will tell you. I can't do that because it's not my personality. Well maybe you ought to make it your personality because the personality that you are allowing yourself to be right now is getting you nowhere in life with your finances, your health, your family, or your friends! What good is it to be the most popular person in the graveyard… or the trailer park? Could everyone achieve a huge financial level of success? The answer is–"absolutely." Why won't they? Ask them. I don't want to hear their whining so I stopped asking. I've asked so many young people what they want to be or do and 90% of them tell me they want to own their own business. I hear everything from owning a salon to starting a computer repair business and everything in between.

Fear will keep most of them from doing anything. Fear is what will keep you from reaching your dreams. By the way, dreams are nothing more than goals with deadlines. Dreams are the big picture, and goals represent the plan you create to get there. But fear will paralyze you every time. Fear will keep the investor from buying a piece of property. Fear will keep a prospective business owner from taking the plunge and starting a business. Fear will keep you off of Wall Street. The reason you are afraid is because you don't know for sure what's going to happen. That's a fear of the unknown, and the only way to eliminate the fear of the unknown is to make it known. You do that through educating yourself. It is your responsibility to do that. I don't care if everybody you know failed in business, lost thousands in the stock market, or owned property that tenants didn't pay. Maybe they didn't educate themselves enough. And if they did educate themselves enough and that happened, I'm sure they're not whining about it right now because the other twenty properties they own are doing great! That's why I love the object of Robert Kiyosaki and the Rich Dad series. His goal is to educate people and increase their financial literacy. When I say that fear will paralyze you, I mean that fear will make you not do anything. Actually, you will do something, but it will hurt you rather than help you. By doing nothing, that is doing something. It's the implementation of a poor plan that ends in defeat every time.

Overcoming my fear of the unknown is what the writing of this book is for me. I've always wanted to write and speak, but fear kept me from doing it. Fear said that I wasn't good enough. Fear said that no one would listen. Fear said that no one would buy the book, and that it would be a waste of time, energy, and money. My fear paralyzed me. I did nothing. I didn't write the book. That is, until I was able to overcome my fear. So what fear do you need to overcome to achieve your goals? Is it fear of what other people will think? Is it the fear of losing money? Is it the fear of making a commitment? Is it the fear of just not knowing what's going to happen next? Then listen up, because this is how you get over it. You educate yourself. If you are scared of buying property, then read every book on real estate, listen to every tape, and go to every seminar on the subject. If you aren't sure you can start and run a successful business, then educate yourself. Read books, listen to other successful business owners, ask them questions, and get around winners as much as you possibly can to hear what they have to say. What eventually happens is it becomes second nature to you. I remember when I couldn't play a musical instrument. It was intimidating sitting down in front of one. That is, until I learned to play it, then it wasn't fearful anymore. I was afraid of high school until I went to junior high and realized that I knew what I needed to know for high school. Educating yourself will help you eliminate your fear of the unknown every single time! You wanted a secret to success, there it is. Overcome your fear. Fear will keep you from your dreams every single time. Fear will keep you from getting the man or woman that you want to date or marry. Fear will keep you from making money. Fear will keep you from getting the position that you've always wanted. Fear will keep you from starting a business. Fear will keep you from investing. Fear will keep you from talking to the people you need to talk to in order to accomplish your plan. Fear will keep you from losing weight. Fear will keep you from being the person you were meant to become. Fear is no respecter of persons. It doesn't matter who you are, you have to learn to overcome fear.

That's why it is a major source of irritation for me when I hear someone say, "Well, that's just who I am" or "That's my personality. I can't help it." That's bologna. That's a cop out.

You can be whomever you choose to be. You aren't shy; you're scared. You can become whoever and whatever you want to be, but you get to choose. You can help it. You can be more outgoing. You can tone it down a bit if you are overbearing. One of my mentors once said to me, "You know, Rollan, when you're a hammer, everything looks like a nail." You can laugh more. You can be more serious. You can like people. You can get the capital you need. You can lose the weight. You can be a nicer, sweeter, more pleasant person to be around. You can be more studious. You can be more accommodating. It is within your power to do so. I can't wait until a little later when I talk to you about how to use the power that everyone has. I don't like whining, complaining, excuses (I don't make em'; I don't take em'!), or laziness.

## *Reflections on the Riches from this Chapter*

- Thought is the only tangible thing from which anything is created.

- You choose to be who you are, and you have chosen where you are currently.

- Dreams are nothing more than goals with deadlines.

- When you're a hammer, everything looks like a nail.

# Chapter 2

# YOU HAVE THE RIGHT–
# TO CHOOSE

I t's your choice. Go ahead and choose. Where do you want to live? Where do you want to go to school? Where do you want to travel and vacation? Who do you want your friends to be? Who do you want to date or marry? What kind of business do you want to start? How much money do you want to have? How much do you want your assets to be worth? How much monthly and yearly income do you desire? What kind of automobiles do you want? What kind of house do you want to live in? Where would you like to have more homes? What kind of boat or yacht would you like? What would you do with a multi-million dollar custom-made coach? What would the interior colors be in your personal Boeing 747? What charities would you give too? How much do you want to be able to give? What kind of scholarships would you like to create?

It's your choice. You get to control your circumstances. That's right. You control 95% of what happens to you by the choices you make. That means that the choices you make today, this month, and this year will affect the "circumstances" you are in a year from now. It's your choice. All the questions I just asked are things you can control. You are where you are financially right now because that is where you chose to be by the previous decisions you made. You are where you are mentally and emotionally right now because that is exactly where you chose to be by the number of books, tapes, mentors, and conferences you have chosen to partake in. You are where you are spiritually right now because that's where you chose to be. You are where you are geographically right now because that is where you chose to be. You say, "My job moved me. I didn't choose to live here." You chose to live there when you moved. You could have resigned. Your company didn't have the FBI cart you and your belongings to "no-man's land." You willingly went! People who continually complain about the snow in the North or the heat in the South can choose to change that. If they choose not to change their circumstances, then they elect to lose their right to complain.

My mother always taught me that you are the same person today that you'll be five years from now except for two things: the books you read and the people you meet. You see, I believe that you can have your cake and eat it too because I believe in the law of sowing and reaping. This is the law of cause and effect. I believe that every action has a reaction or consequence, whether it is good or bad. I believe that if I sow corn seed, I'm going to get corn. If I plant an apple tree, I'm going to get apples. To say that you can't control your circumstances is to say that you can plant an apple tree and not really know what type of fruit it will yield. That violates a law of nature. Your life truly is a Hollywood movie, and you are the director, producer, and the cast. You're the make-up artist and stunt man. The best part is you get to write your own ending. None of us had much to do with our beginning. We didn't do too much to bring ourselves into this world. We didn't write a letter requesting our lives or anything like that. But we do have a free will that has been given to us by the Almighty. I can tell you with absolute certainty that just as planting an apple tree will bring you apples, so making the right decisions, including the decision to eliminate fear, procrastination, and laziness, allow you to reap quality results. This decision will produce better circumstances for your life. I can have the life and ending that I want because I get to control my circumstances. I have dedicated an entire chapter to teaching you how to control your circumstances.

Because of your free will, you choose where you live, what kind of car you drive, etc. I remember when I chose to live in Florida. I lived in Knoxville, Tennessee at the time, and I had a full time job. I didn't see how in the world I would be able to move with my family. There were too many variables that would need to be worked out and obstacles to overcome. But whether I stayed in Tennessee or moved to Florida was my choice. I chose the latter. I didn't say it was easy to make this choice. In fact, it meant I'd have to work a lot harder before things got better. It meant that we would go through a period of transition. But that's not the point. The point is to have the life you want, to be in the geographical location you desire, and to be whom you want to be. That's what makes you happy; it's being who you want to be. You are happy when you are content with who you are. Rich or poor is not the point. Fat or skinny isn't the issue. Tall or short has nothing to do with it. The point is to be the best you can be, and most people are not the best they can be in every area of their life. They choose not to read today. They choose not to listen to informational and motivational media. They choose not to spend their "free time" educating themselves under the tutelage of a competent mentor at seminars and conferences. We are a result of the choices that we've made. But just as we are a result of our past choices, we can choose to change. We can choose to start reading the right kind of books. We can choose to start bettering ourselves during our driving time through the use of audiotapes or CD's. Brian Tracy said, "The radio is chewing gum for the ears." Turn your car into a "university on wheels," he concluded.

Lack of money is not an excuse or reason. The only fact is that you choose to work on you or you choose not to work on you. You chose to go eat ice cream when you were trying to lose weight. You chose to go out instead of invest the time into your business. You chose to work at the job you complain about. They didn't put a gun to your head and make you accept that level of pay. You accepted it. You said yes. It was your choice. So quit complaining that you don't make enough money. Do something about it. Choose to change. Choose to change your finances. Choose to change your health and eating habits. Choose to change the quality of your family life and your marriage. Choose to change how you rear your kids if you don't like what you've created. Choose to change how much time you spend with those you love. Choose to turn your liabilities into assets. Choose to change your spending habits and where you spend your time and whom you give your time to.

You don't spend time; you invest it. You invest your time like you invest your money. The lesson here is to choose whom you invest your time in wisely. Don't gamble with your time. Invest it. Don't just "let it happen." Make it happen. Plan your schedule. Use a palm pilot, BlackBerry, day-timer, or planner, and schedule your time. Don't let the person that just called you determine if and how long you talk to them. You control that. You control how much time you spend with people. You are in control. The reason I'm harping on this subject is because of the vast misconception of a phrase that has permeated our society that goes, "I'm busy" or "I don't have time." You've got just as much time as the next guy. That's pure genius. Yes, I know you are busy. Who isn't? You are busy with what you want to be busy with, and I'm busy with what I want to be busy with. I don't want to be busy working for somebody else. That's just me. I know your job is demanding, but do a better job scheduling yourself. Educate yourself on how to get organized. Educate yourself to cut out the time wasters that are in everyone's day.

Why do we say we can't do something because we don't have time instead of being men and women of integrity and saying, "Well, I would do that, but I just don't want to" or "I don't think that's the wisest investment of my time. I can get a higher return on investment and yield by investing my time over here." Oh, I know. You don't want to hurt anybody's feelings. You are afraid of hurting someone. You're concerned with how they will think of you. My mentor once told me that when I tell other people my problems, the majority of people don't care (because they have their own problems they're consumed with) and the rest of the people are glad it is happening to me. If something is not in my best interest or in the best interest of my family, then I have learned to say "no." Why do I say "no?"—because I choose to say "no." And that's the key. We have chosen what takes up our time. We have chosen what we spend our money on. Even creditors don't torture you to make you pay your monthly mortgage. You choose to send that check in, pay by phone, or pay online because you want to keep your credit clean. We have chosen what and how we make decisions. Yet, it is your choice where you are this time next year financially, physically, emotionally, professionally, socially, and spiritually. Choose carefully.

*Reflection on the Riches from this Chapter*

- You can have your cake and eat it too if you believe in the law of sowing and reaping and sow what it is you desire.

- You are happy when you are content with who you are.

- You don't spend time; you invest it.

*Chapter 3*

# CONTROL YOUR CIRCUMSTANCES

"Can you control your circumstances?" The answer I get most often when I ask this question is astounding. Most people do not believe that you can control your circumstances. The majority of people think that this is impossible. That's why I'm writing to the 5% (and those that want to be 5%'ers) because the other 95% thinks you cannot control your circumstances, but to get where you're going, you better be able to control your circumstances or you'll never get there! We need it to be possible. One might say, "But wait, I didn't make that hurricane come through and destroy everything I had." Well, you chose to live where hurricanes have a tendency to visit, didn't you? You chose to under-insure yourself instead of over-insure. Again I hear, "But wait, I didn't choose to lose my home in foreclosure or bankruptcy." Yes you did, when your nose was running and you called in sick to work. Yes you did, when you chose to eat out instead of eating at home. Yes you did, when you decided not to work. Yet another says, "But wait, I can't control if someone likes me or not." Yes you can, by how you treat them; how you talk to them; the time you invest in them, and what you do for them. No matter what baggage, I mean circumstances, you think you couldn't have controlled, you're wrong. You could have done more, spent more time with them, saved more, invested more, and planned better. You are where you are because you chose to be there and that's the dirty truth (or the good news!).

My mentor always told me that there are only two types of people I should hang around and spend my time with–people who want what I have and those that have what I want; people who want the kind of marriage I have and those who have the kind of marriage I want; people who are financially where I want to be and those that want to be where I'm at financially; people who are where I want to be spiritually and those that want to have a close spiritual walk. This rule has been golden to help me evaluate who my friends are and if I continue to invest time with them.

With all the people losing their jobs today, one is most certain to say, "How could I have controlled that circumstance?" Actually, that's probably how I wish they would ask it! Well, considering the fact that you are reading a book where the author has experienced that firsthand, let me say that you and I could have controlled that circumstance. "That's incredulous," you exclaim! Not really. First of all, we could have looked at the track record of the company. Then we could have looked at the trends that affect business to see where our industry was headed. Then we could have looked at the role our company played within our industry. Then we could have looked at the tell-tale signs. You know, things like creditors calling the office repeatedly and customers dropping like flies, etc. Then we could have started a part time business because we know that even though a company can look great, they still control our finances, and we just can't let someone else decide if we are going to eat next month. No matter how foreseeable point in the future. By the way, if a disaster happened, while I was on the cruise, I still could have controlled that circumstance by not going on that cruise. Or if the ship wrecked on a glacier on an Alaskan cruise, then I could have prevented the glacier circumstance by cruising the Caribbean! Does this mean you don't do anything so nothing bad happens to you? No! It just means you take responsibility for what happens to you and the circumstances that you are in.

Many people do not take personal responsibility for anything anymore. I remember reading in Dale Carnegie's *How To Win Friends & Influence People* about how Thomas "Two-Gun" Crowlie, a murderer who killed innocent people and was responsible for one of the largest manhunts in Chicago history, said that he was a "good person, one that would do no one any harm." Unbelievable, isn't it? Even he wouldn't take responsibility for his actions. Employees blame their employers or other employees. Husbands blame their wives. Wives blame their husbands, and their children blame everyone else. For the most part, people believe they are right the majority of the time. People will admit that they make mistakes, but they rarely accept personal responsibility. It doesn't matter if you were there or not. It doesn't matter if they work specifically for you or not. It doesn't matter if there was anything you could have physically done or not. If it's in your hands now, admit it, apologize for it, claim it, and vow to correct it. Now the guy who does that deserves a raise! Yet, so many people fear disciplinary action if they do that. Truth is, most of the time, management already has a hunch as to who is responsible so when the blame game starts, it's easier to decipher the situation. Accepting responsibility will develop your leadership ability. Those that are truly to blame will see your readiness to accept personal responsibility. The reason is that oftentimes, several people are responsible for the end result. So, because they did not single-handedly ruin whatever it is, they don't take full responsibility. Try something different. The next time something bad happens to you, try accepting personal responsibility. So you lost your house, it's your fault. Don't blame your business, your job, or your spouse's spending. Take personal responsibility. So someone did you wrong and now you don't have money anymore. Accept personal responsibility for it and move on. So they lied to you, take personal responsibility for believing them. You could have chosen not to believe them. So you don't deserve the health problems, accept personal responsibility for your diet, lack of exercise, and smoking.

The first step to controlling your circumstances is to accept personal responsibility for where you are right now at this point in your life. You can't blame others. This is not how you get ahead. That's right. That means you can't blame the economy for where you are financially. You can't blame interest rates for where you're at. You can't blame anything, even if it played a role, for where you are. Accept full responsibility and make it a habit to do so. What a difference it will make in your life. You will find opportunities to do this almost daily and certainly weekly. I have seen some people, though rare, who take this too far to the other extreme, and they cross the line into schmoozing the boss. If you didn't even have a hand in it at all, then it's hard to take the responsibility, unless you're the leader, boss, or manager. For example, if I'm asking the marketing team what went wrong, I don't want the janitor saying, "Well, if I had scrubbed the floor more, then that spot wouldn't have thrown their concentration off." That's the extreme that I'm referring to. I think you understand the difference.

The point is simple. Quit blaming others. Take responsibility. It doesn't matter that someone else had a hand in it, it's your fault, and that's all you need to know and think. Don't let yourself off the hook. That pressure you put on yourself is good for you. It raises the bar for yourself and others. It forces you to get better.

You control your circumstances by taking personal responsibility for the decisions that you make. The more you do this, the better you will get at making decisions (if you learn from your mistakes), thus controlling your circumstances more effectively. I controlled my geographical circumstance by walking into the vice-president's office and telling him that I was moving to Florida and putting in my notice (as I handed it to him). It was simple actually. My car drove the same way it always had to work. I put one leg in front of the other as I walked. I knocked on the door and spoke. It didn't take any special talents or abilities to do this. All it took was a decision that I was willing to accept full responsibility for that action, whether it turned out good or bad. That's how I controlled my geographical circumstance. Most people would not have been willing to do what my family and I did to get to where we are financially. We paid a difficult price (Actually, we didn't. Remember when I said to ask, "Compared to what? Working 40 years for someone else and still being broke?"). We encountered obstacles that few people will ever go through on our success journey. But we got to where we were going, and that's all we cared about. We wanted to control our circumstance. The chapter later on about turning obstacles into opportunities will help you take negative circumstances and turn them into the best things that ever could have happened to you.

*Reflections on the Riches from this Chapter*

- There are only two types of people you should spend time with:

  People who have what you want, and
  People who want what you have

- You can control your circumstances.

- People will admit that they make mistakes, but they will rarely accept personal responsibility for them.

# Chapter 4

# MONEY, MONEY, MONEY

L et's talk about money. I hope I don't offend you, but if I do, it's probably because you don't have any. Frankly, if you are, then I'm surprised you've read this far. I wouldn't expect that one offended with this chapter would ever hope to be a 5%er.

It's true that money doesn't buy happiness. We already talked about how to be happy and having money was not the source. It's true that the LOVE of money is the root of all evil, not money itself. It is also true that money is neither good nor bad in and of itself. It doesn't buy drugs the second it is printed at the Treasury. It doesn't support crime the moment it's created. I've never seen a hundred dollar bill grow legs and go do something bad or illegal. I've only seen good people do good things with money and bad people do bad things with money. It's not what I have that's evil; it's what I love that's evil. Money is not a person. It does not have a will like you and I do. It doesn't have a mind and cannot think or make decisions. It is paper.

It is true that this paper is what you work for and allows you to eat. It determines how safe an environment you live in, and to what extent you are allowed to legally enjoy the comforts of life. If we were able to stay home, have all the food we want, have cable TV, have free medical insurance, and have all our needs met, then we'd be on welfare! Nonetheless, if we were able to do that, then most of us probably would spend our time doing something different than our current jobs. Perhaps we would work on that business we always wanted to start or that book we always wanted to write or the travel we always wanted to take and time we always wanted to spend with family. Money controls the majority of our waking time, and it permeates every aspect of our lives. Our churches want it, and the grocery store wants it. What's more is that if you watch the majority of people at the grocery store, you'll see them adding up prices, checking to see if they can get something for five cents cheaper. Some folks even have to put things back! That's not how I want to go grocery shopping.

So what does it take to be rich? Super wealthy? Incredibly wealthy? Ultra-wealthy? Is it an idea? Is it being in the right place at the right time? Does it take an element of luck?

Believe it or not, achieving wealth is not an elusive mastery. It is a matter of sowing and reaping. It is a matter of honoring and utilizing the laws of nature (including compounding). The law of compounding and multiplication can be seen in nature. Animals breed to produce offspring–and most don't have just one baby! Flower seeds are transported through various insects and even the wind (dandelions). One seed can have countless number of plants or trees. There are specific principles that cater to wealth. They must be learned. They are not inherent. They do not come naturally; they must be acquired. This knowledge is readily available for the person that diligently seeks after it. Wealth is attracted to those who respect it.

There are so many technical books to give you skills you need to be an expert investor in whichever asset(s) you choose. It's not just about that. You have to have a general working knowledge of how money works. I can tell you that at some point, to go from nothing to vast supply, you will have a financial turning point. There will be one investment or situation that you will look back on and say, "That was the turning point." It might be a deal that provided you the necessary cash flow to go on to bigger and better assets. It might have been a business break-through. It might have been one customer, one business partner, one client, one contact, one prospect, or one order. What creates that one investment that can be used as a springboard to financial freedom and success? I submit to you that it is different for everybody. There are as many different scenarios as there are success stories. For me, it was a real estate deal structured so that it immediately gave me tens of thousands of dollars. Of course, I bought a business and invested in paper assets as well, while still owning and controlling the property. This was my personal springboard. It was software for Bill Gates and a dilapidated hotel for Donald Trump. If your "turning point" hasn't happened yet, don't despair. Your continual self-development and financial education will allow you to see the opportunity that no one else sees at that moment, and you will be able to capitalize on it. The funny thing is that you may or may not even know what it will be! I didn't know if my break-through would happen through my business, real estate, or paper investments. And what makes you break-through in one area and me in another is that our levels of education are higher in different areas. You are more comfortable investing in one place because you are more educated and know the different options you have in structuring a business deal, concept, or idea. You have to be continually looking for your opportunity and be intensely, mentally preoccupied (this should not be visual to others)

*Reflection on the Riches from this Chapter*

🖙 I have never seen a hundred dollar bill grow legs and go
do something bad or illegal. I have only seen good people do good things with money and bad people do bad
things with money.

🖙 Wealth is attracted to those who respect it.

🖙 There will be one investment or situation that you will
look back on and say, "That was my turning point."

🖙 Your continual self-development and financial education
will allows you to see the opportunity that no one else
sees at that moment and you will be able to capitalize
on it.

*Chapter 5*

# SECRET TO GETTING MORE

B efore we emphasize some things you can work on to breathe the breath of life into your vision, I want you to first understand something you must be in order to be successful. You must be a giver. This makes no sense, but it makes all the sense in the world! Think about it. If I want money, I'm supposed to give money away. If I want time, I'm supposed to give time away. If I want a better marriage, I have to be a better husband. If I want a better job, I have to be a better employee. If I want to achieve more, I have to take on more tasks. If you want more of something, you must first give it away. This eternal principle is timeless. When I sow a seed, I always ask God to bless it one thousand fold, ten thousand fold, one hundred thousand fold.

The law of giving is based on the law of sowing and reaping which we talked about in an earlier chapter. If I want apples, I plant an apple tree. If I want money, I sow a financial seed. Seeds are made to grow into something much larger and greater than itself. Look at the mighty oak tree and the little acorn. Now look at how many acorns one oak tree can produce. It is amazing. You take the one seed you have and plant it, expecting your harvest full of acorns. In order to live the life you want, you must learn to give. This is something that we must learn to some degree depending on where our capacity for giving is currently. As a baby, we are selfish. We want mommy's attention. As we grow up, we want the biggest piece of cake, and we want things done our way, and we tend to be selfish. We think mainly of ourselves.

This is probably why the majority of people are where they are. They have never learned to give from their hearts. You must be a cheerful giver. If you give grudgingly, then it's not giving. Cheerful giving is the only way to give or you shouldn't give at all. Cheerful giving isn't only cheerful because it might be a tax write-off. Give when it's not a write-off. Think a little bit more generously than that. As Robert Kiyosaki said, "You can get rich by being cheap. The only problem is once you're rich, you're still cheap! And nobody likes cheap rich people!" I couldn't have said it any better. Prosperity is determined by how much you can give while keeping a smile on your face.

This law of life will heap more money, time, goodness, gifts, and prosperity in your life than you will be able to handle. Recently, I was so worn out because of all the good things that happened to me. At one point, I didn't think my heart could handle it. I sure didn't know what I was going to do if things kept getting better! Every time I give and sow a seed into another individual's life, I claim that seed and proclaim a harvest. I ask for the harvest I want. I don't plant a seed without expecting a crop, and I don't sow a financial seed without expecting a financial harvest.

My question to you is this. How many seeds have you planted today? How many seeds have you planted into the lives of other people this week? It really is a game. Let's see who can plant the most seeds. He who sows the most seeds wins. If you want more time, you must make a time investment. I remember when I had zippo money. I had a few dollars in my pocket and that was it. I won't ever forget a little girl coming by selling candy bars, and I gave her the $4 dollars I had to buy candy bars. As she walked off of my front porch, I claimed a financial harvest from my seed. It doesn't make much sense, does it? If I don't have much left, it seems like I should hold onto it. But that's not the way it works. When I need money, I start giving more generously than before. I realize that not being generous enough is what caused my lack in the first place. My wife and I take college kids out to eat every Sunday to nice restaurants. One of the girls had never been to a nice restaurant before. We sow this financial seed into their lives each Sunday, with no tax advantage, but we claim an unbelievable harvest. We have been more blessed since we made this a habit than ever before. In fact, there were Sundays when we barely had enough money to feed ourselves, much les anybody else. The students looked forward to it so much that we knew we had to plant another seed. That's one thing you learn pretty quickly as well. You can't ever quit planting seeds. You actually become a farmer. You can't stop. Well, you can, but you don't have a crop for much longer and then you have a financial drought because you failed to plant seeds of graciousness and plenteousness in the lives of those around you.

I spent several hours with some friends of ours last Saturday afternoon and evening. I planted the seed of time and money into their lives so that one day, I will be planting seeds of time and money with my friends on my 100' yacht. Don't expect to get if you're not willing to give. You don't get before you give either. That's like standing in front of the fireplace and saying that you won't put wood in it until you get warm. That's like the people who won't start a business until they

*Reflection on the Riches from this Chapter*

- Prosperity is determined by how much you can give while keeping a smile on your face.

- You can't ever quit planting seeds.

- Don't expect to get if you're not willing to give.

- Your harvest doesn't necessarily come from the place you plant the seed.

*Chapter 6*

# FINANCIAL CODE RED

On Success Lane, you will undoubtedly hit some potholes because this road is always under construction. You are sure to encounter detours and your trip is sure to take you longer than you anticipated. That's okay. The point is that you get there and that you arrive in one piece. That's what this chapter is all about. How do you get there and keep your sanity?

With every opportunity comes opposition. Any time you willingly place yourself in a transition phase, you will self-induce stress. Success is built on inconvenience. It's not always comfortable. If you're building a business, you will surely know what it feels like to be strapped for cash. You will know what it feels like to sit down one day or evening and wonder why you ever decided to embark on this adventure. You will definitely question your sanity along the line. You will know what defeat tastes like. You will know what losing smells like. You will know what losers look like. You will know how it feels to think you're finished.

But you will also know that the only difference between winners and losers is that the winner got up just one more time. He kept getting back up. Nothing kept him down forever. Winning isn't about not getting knocked down. Losing is about staying down. Winning is about getting back up. The Proverbs tell us that a righteous man gets knocked down seven times and riseth up again. My reality is not my current circumstances; it's my dream. That's where I live. You're not going to be able to grab a hold of your dream if you're still holding on to your past disappointments.

Let me first help eliminate a few potholes. We can't discard all of them, but there are several that we can send to the recycle bin. It will help you to realize that you get whatever you focus on. Have you ever been driving along, noticed a pothole, and purposefully tried to avoid it by staring at it only to still hit it? Why is that? It is because that's what you focused on. You get in life what you focus on. That's why it's so important not to focus on what you don't want to happen, but rather focus on what you do want to happen. Yes, you should make lemonade when life hands you a lemon.

No matter what obstacle I'm presented with or what problem I am faced with, I first realize that there is a seed of opportunity equal to or greater than the problem or obstacle. Every cloud does have a silver lining, and I believe that I can come out of each obstacle with greater prosperity, greater insights, and increased power and position because of it. People don't realize what a great leader you are during the good times. It takes a crisis for people to see who the man is. Look at September 11, 2001. Now you may have heard of Mayor Rudolph Giuliani, but you didn't know him then like you know him now. Why? Because people found out what he was made of in the aftermath of 9/11/01. And that's the way it is with us. You have to be looking for the good in the situation. However, I will say, if it wasn't meant to be your blessing, don't take it as your curse either. Now, if this is my belief going into any difficult situation, I am in a much better mental position to turn my lemon into lemonade.

Alright, now for the number one practical thing I can do when faced with a challenge. I heard Dexter Yager, a multi-millionaire businessman that has greatly influenced my life, say one time, "It's not what happens; it's how you handle it." That statement gets me through every challenge I am ever faced with by understanding that in every problem, there is a seed that I can use to increase my wealth or wisdom. That mentality, coupled with the fact that the challenge or the incident that occurred only accounts for about 5% of what happens, will help you shape the other 95%. That's how you handle a situation to control the circumstance. I hope that makes sense. When something goes wrong or something bad happens, most people make it worse by their reaction. They say something harsh. They retaliate. Their actions are irreversible. And they end up taking a bad situation and making it ten times worse. What I'm saying is that it's not what happens; it's how you handle it. Impatience can ruin a business deal. You want to know right now because the silence is killing you, so you bug the person one more time instead of giving them time. Your call seals the decision for them. Time and again, impatience has cost me clients, prospects, or sales. It wasn't what happened that killed the deal; it's how I handled what happened that killed the deal. That goes back to personal responsibility. I can't blame the killed deal on anyone else but myself.

When things go south, most people react. And their first reaction is normally not the best one they could have chosen. When I received the news that our company went under, I was shocked. However, I immediately regained my composure, put a smile on my face (after the meeting in which I told my employees) and walked out. Why? Because I knew that it's not what just happened that mattered, it's how I handled it. I could let this ruin me, or I could make this the best thing that ever happened to me. I had just closed the week before on another expensive home. My monthly mortgages on my two homes were over $4,000 a month. Now I had no job. It isn't hard to see what could have happened had I not handled what happened properly. All I'm saying is that people who have a lot of drama in their life create 95% of that drama. Now they will deny it to the hilt, but it's true. They created it by how they handled the first 5% that was out of their control–or what they thought was out of their control. That's why I don't like it when speakers and authors say, "I think this, and I think that." I always want to say, "I don't care what you think. I care what you know." People are where they are because they thought this would happen or they thought things would turn out this way. People think all sorts of things, but you have to learn what people know. And you have to be able to separate fact from fiction. You have to be able to discern fact from opinion and truth from point of view. That's why you can have two witnesses see the same crime and both give different accounts of it. We can all look at a picture and say what it looks like to us, and we would come up with different answers. So what seems like truth to you doesn't seem like truth to me and so on. Your success will depend on your ability to discern the differences in people in these areas.

That's why I love to watch people. I learn so much from just sitting and watching people. You can see what their life is like by the look on their face. You can tell the people that have had a hard life. You can tell the people that have never worked a day in their life. You can tell the happy-go-lucky young people who have never had to pay a bill. You can tell those that get bogged down with relationship problems. The point here is that it's not what happens; it's how you handle it The next time a crisis comes in your life, remember that 95% of what happens will be determined by how you react and handle the problem. Act—don't react.

*Reflection on the Riches from this Chapter*

- Success is built on inconvenience.

- The only difference between winners and losers is that the winner gets up one more time.

- My reality is not my current circumstances; it's my dream. That's where I live.

- You get in life what you focus on (so don't focus on potholes!).

- There is a seed of opportunity equal to or great than the problem or obstacle that you encounter.

- You have to be able to discern fact from opinion and truth from point of view.

# Chapter 7

# KEY TO SUCCESS
# AND FAILURE

I 'll never forget the tape I heard from Earl Nightingale that taught me the lesson that changed the way I think forever. He said that the key to success and the key to failure are the same thing. The same key that will lead you to a fabulous life is the same key that will drive a man into the gutter. The same law that will make you rich can make you poor. The same law will make you a fortune that will make you a pauper. The key to success and the key to failure is you become what you think about.

Proverbs tells us many things about controlling our mind, but one sticks out to me. It goes, "As a man thinketh in his heart, so is he." You become what you think about. Mr. Nightingale did not discover a new truth fifty years ago. This timeless principle has been around for ages. Your thoughts will determine who and what you become. If you think like a coward, you will act like a coward. If you think negatively, you will be a negative person. If you think about nonsense, your life will simply drift. That's one of the most devastating plagues of the last quarter century. It's not HIV. It's not cancer. It is that people don't think. They don't know how to think. We are not taught in schools to think. We are taught to memorize. That's why so many have a difficult time in college, besides the fact that they lack self-discipline. They haven't learned to think. Thinking is hard work. Thinking will wear you out. Your mind is your greatest asset and can produce more money than you know what to do with. And once you learn to think, you must learn to think right. There is a difference. Most people simply repeat what they've heard someone else say that sounded good to them. That's right. Most people are parrots. They echo and repeat what they hear others say, and they say it so often that they eventually believe they thought of it and came to that conclusion on their own. They think they are thinking. Your mother taught you this, remember? She said, "If you tell a lie long enough, eventually you'll believe it yourself." The media today can harp on things so long and shape your thoughts to the point that you believe you came to that conclusion based on facts, but the truth is that your failure to control what you allowed your mind to think about allowed outside forces to plant seeds in your mind to bring you to certain pre-drawn conclusions. If I ask you the right questions, I can get you to say what I want you to say, and you'd think it was your idea. This is so powerful. You must learn to control your mind.

Here's a test. I want you to stop reading for ten minutes. I want you to think of a problem or crisis in your life right now, and I want you to think of nothing but solutions for that problem for ten straight minutes. The first time your mind thinks of a phrase that is off of the subject, start the ten minutes over. I can tell you that this will certainly take some practice and rarely will someone even reach one minute on the first time. Controlling your mind is a discipline that is learned. It does not come naturally. Think about when you were in church or a meeting of some sort and a speaker was speaking. Have you ever found yourself thinking about what the speaker was talking about and then it goes from that to how it relates to something recent in your life? From there you think of what you're going to do that afternoon and on to what you're going to eat and with whom? It is amazing. Our minds wonder naturally. What I want you to do is control your mind. You get to choose the type of thoughts and the subject of what you want to think about. This doesn't go just for this ten minutes, it goes for your entire life. If you become what you think about and it can make you billions of dollars or ruin you financially and in every other way, it's of paramount importance that you learn to do this. Your ability to control your mind will determine how big a business you are able to build. Your ability to control your mind will determine the size bank account that you can successfully manage. Your ability to control your mind will determine your leadership capability and how many people you can effectively lead.

To achieve the level of success that I believe you want to achieve, you must not allow your mind to wander. The first step is to realize that you do have control over what you think. Despite popular opinion, thoughts don't just happen. In fact, thought is the only tangible source from which anything is created. Buildings don't build themselves. Someone thought about it at some point. They imagined it. They had a vision of what they wanted. Their thought formed their reality. This is what others call luck or the Midas touch. I don't have the Midas touch; I have just learned how to control my thinking to accomplish the goals that I have set.

There are many reasons why taking ten minutes to think about possible solutions for a challenge you are currently facing is helpful. One of the reasons is that you can receive guidance from the Omnipotent One. I have received some brilliant ideas during this time of silence, reflection, and meditation that I would never claim as my own. Last week, I placed myself in the silence and meditation and within 30 minutes I had an idea. I told my wife not to get too excited, but I had an idea. Within three days, I had received a $10,000 check from my one idea. Oh, the power of a thought. It will cost you a lot of money not to learn how to control your mind.

You must also learn where you think best. Where are you able to block out the commotion of life and just meditate? You must find what scenery best enables you to enter into silence. You must learn to control your mind while you are in this place to bring the ideas to you to build your success and to accomplish your goals. This has been my secret to building a successful business. This has been my secret to staying focused on my dream. I believe, as Mike Murdock once said, that the only reason men fail is broken focus. Most people can't stay focused because they can't control their mind. They can't control what they think about. I'm telling you that you can control every thought you have if you just make it a priority and not allow yourself to cheat.

It's not what you know; it's how you think that makes you a success. You shouldn't take your dreams to heaven with you, and you sure shouldn't die with your dreams still in you. But you will if you don't learn to control how you think. 87% of the thoughts you think are negative, and you think between 40–50,000 thoughts per day. The vast majority of what you tell yourself is negative self-talk. That's not the way to live; in fact, it's a sure way to die. No one ever achieved their dream by telling themselves they couldn't do it. When your dream becomes your focus, you will be unstoppable. Until you reach that point, you will think goal-setting doesn't work. You will think that you can't have your cake and eat it too. You will think that success just wasn't meant for you or that you dream too big. That's impossible. When God gives you a dream, it will be one that you can't achieve the way you are now. You must become the person that can achieve it. Knowledge doesn't have power unless you use it, and you can't use it without thinking. The biggest challenge you'll face on the trail of success is your own stupidity.

The key to success and the key to failure is you become what you think about. So what do you think about the majority of the time? Do you constantly blame yourself for not having accomplished more by your age? Do you constantly beat yourself up for not saying this or that at the right moment or by not doing something? Do you constantly talk about the million dollar deal that you passed up only to continue passing more up? I saw this last week in some friends of mine. We were looking at a condo on the beach that was selling for $800,000, and they only had to put down $80,000 cash right then and a 10% letter of credit from the bank, and they wouldn't close on it for a year. Based on the last eighteen months, they would have been able to sell their pre-construction penthouse after closing for around $1.7 million dollars! They had the cash, but they kept talking about the deals like this that they had passed up over their lifetime and sure enough, they passed this one up too. By the way, it sold that afternoon to someone who wasn't going to let it pass them up. Life is full of these examples and the only way for you to not be an example like this is to control your mind. You can't afford to think poverty thoughts. You can't afford to think, "I can't afford this." You can't afford to think that it won't work for you. You can't afford to doubt your ability to succeed in business, family, and in life. If you don't control your mind then you are a puppet because someone is thinking for you. They are thinking about how they can control what you think. Learn to think. This is the only thing that will guarantee your success. You can have your very own insurance policy that you will succeed by controlling your mind and what you think. Will you do it? For the sake of your success, and that of your family, will you do it? Do you have the courage to do it? Will you take on this full time job of controlling your thoughts and not thinking about something just because someone brought it up? Most people think about whatever is brought up at the supper table. Most people engage in conversation at work on their lunch break, and they are allowing 95%'ers to control what they think about on their lunch break. That's lunacy! They are letting someone who is no where near where they want to be and has no plans of getting there to control what topics they think about. You didn't choose to think about that. They brought it up and now you're thinking about it. Politically correct answers are the enemy of thinking.

I have not met a man yet that wouldn't defend his own home from an un-welcomed intruder. He would fight to the best of his ability if an intruder came into his home. But I find that 95% of American households don't stop the robber who takes their mind. They lock the doors on their car and house so no one will steal anything and then they take the robber to the most precious, most expensive, most valuable thing that any of us have in the world, our minds. We give them our minds. We won't let anyone take the cheap stuff in life, but we have given them our best so they don't have to take it. It's like a thief coming into your home and stealing your jewelry, and as he's on his way out, you stop him and say, "Oh, let me show you where to look. You forgot to take the money out of the secret vault." That's what we do when we allow others to control what we think. Perhaps we don't realize how valuable our greatest asset is, but if you had to pay for it, you'd realize it. Instead, it has been given to you. Use it; don't abuse it. Guard it; don't let just anybody into your mind. Don't let someone consume your thoughts unless you allow it and don't allow it unless it moves you closer to your goal.

The key to your success or the key to your failure will be that you become what you think about. Oh, I can't portray your thoughts onto a big screen TV for the world to see right now, but everyone will know shortly and in due time. Your life will tell us what you were truly thinking, not just what you said you were thinking. Some people try to speak positively and think negatively and their life will go nowhere and then one will say that it didn't work. But you will know what they were thinking, despite what they were saying outwardly. Your thoughts will form your reality. They are the only reality. What you are going through right now is temporary. Where are you going? Your current thoughts will give you the right answer. Choose your destiny by choosing your thoughts. Guard your heart and mind for out of it are the issues of life.

*Reflection on the Riches from this Chapter*

- ⌇ They key to success and the key to failure is you become what you think about.

- ⌇ Your mind is your greatest asset and can produce more money than you know what to do with.

- ⌇ Once you learn to think, you must learn to think right.

- ⌇ It's not what you know; it's how you think that makes you a success.

- ⌇ You can't afford to think, "I can't afford this."

- ⌇ Politically correct answers are the enemy of thinking.

*Chapter 8*

# MAGIC OF BELIEF

**B**efore I just let loose here in the next few chapters, I want to let you know the biggest reason for my success. This chapter must follow the previous simply because they go hand in hand. If I just controlled my mind that would be great, but this chapter will teach you what to think. What kind of thoughts should I be thinking if I want to prosper in wealth, health, spirituality, and emotionally?

Fortunately, all the guesswork has been taken out. There is no mystery. It is another law of success. Now this law affects every other law, and it touches every area of your life right now. It decides to what level you succeed. It determines the amount of your income. It controls the heights of success you attain. It is the law of belief. It is this law that makes you sick. It is this law that makes you well again. It is this law that makes you prosperous. It is this law that determines if you fail. The law of belief will dictate to what extent you reach your goals.

The question you must ask yourself here is, "Do you believe?" Do you believe in belief? Do you believe that your belief will determine how far you go? Do you believe? Do you believe that you are able and capable? Do you believe that there is no one like yourself to succeed? Do you believe that you have inherited the seeds of greatness? Do you believe that you possess all the talents and skills necessary to be who you were created to be? Do you believe that you will achieve your dreams? Do you believe?

Or do you believe that this deal won't go through because the last several didn't go through? Do you believe that the car won't start because, after all, you can't afford a new car? Do you believe that if something can go wrong, it will? Do you believe that you have bad luck?

I heard an employee once say, "Well, knowing my luck…" I said, "Stop right there." She was telling me how she believed without realizing it. She believed that if something bad was going to happen, it would happen to her because she thought she had bad luck. And she was saying this without even realizing it. If she heard of someone else getting in a wreck at a certain intersection then she probably would too. If someone else got the flu, she'd probably catch it as well because she always got the bugs that went around the office. And sure enough, she'd catch whatever was going around, but only because she believed that she would. But how many people say things like this and think this way? I have always believed that I would not get sick and that I would not catch what is going around and if I did, I believed I didn't really have it. It was my body putting up a great fight to ward off the illness or infection. I refused to believe that I was sick, so my body didn't act sick. It didn't know any better. My belief can shape what happens. I hear people say that they catch a cold every fall and at the beginning of every spring. One reason they catch a cold every year is because they expect themselves to catch it. It's a shame the number of people who get depressed around the holidays because they "always get depressed around the holidays."

They do it because others do it, and they do it because they've always done it. Everything can be controlled by belief.

The good news is that you have the power to change your belief. You must realize the amount of power that belief has in this world. It puts people in power, and it takes people out of power. It brings people together, and it separates the closest of friends. Belief can make the impossible happen for either good or evil. It can even break the laws of nature. It is the only law that has this much power. I don't want you to just take my word on the importance of belief. The Bible says "If thou canst believe, all things are possible to him that believeth." It says IF you can believe, not if you say you believe, but there's an element of doubt. It says if you believe, then all things are possible. The phrase "that's impossible" is heard everyday in our society in business and relationships, but it is incorrect. Nothing is truly impossible. Every law has its roots in this law of belief. The law of sowing and reaping and the law of life itself find their roots in the law of belief. Your level of belief will make the difference between wealth and poverty, happiness and sorrow, and success and failure. You can't just hope something is going to work out. Hope is not a strategy. You have to believe. The Bible also says, "If you have the faith as a grain of mustard seed, ye shall say unto this mountain, 'Be thou removed to yonder place and… nothing shall be impossible unto you.' If you just had a little bit of belief, you could actually contradict the law of gravity and of nature itself. It also says along the same lines that "whosoever shall say unto this mountain 'Be thou removed and be thou cast into the sea, and shall not doubt in his heart, but shall believe that those things which he saith shall come to pass; he shall have whatsoever he saith'." There is power in the tongue–whatsoever he saith. You can speak your way to success. I have experienced this numerous times in my own life. I will type what it is I'm expecting and believing to happen, and I'll hang it on the fridge, in the bathroom, on the mirror, next to my bed, and on the TV. This elevates my belief level and helps me control my mind throughout the day. It also helps me decide what to think about.

Are you saying that my belief could actually pay my bills? That's exactly what I'm saying. Are you saying that my belief can build my business larger than I ever imagined? That's what I'm saying. Are you saying that my belief could help me get over my illness and poor health? Yes. I'm saying that nothing is impossible to you except you must believe it to be so. The power of belief will set you free. This is the truth that is talked about when you hear, "You shall know the truth and the truth shall set you free." There is freedom in the truth of belief. It is the basis for everything good that happens in this world, and it is the basis for everything bad that happens in this world. We are governed by belief. People believe many things, and it is this pattern of belief that makes the world what it is today. We have electricity and lights because someone believed. We have indoor plumbing and not holes in the ground because someone believed. We have transmitted images and information via a TV screen and computers because someone believed. We drive automobiles because someone believed. We have incredibly talented musicians because someone believed. We have incredibly talented sports stars because someone believed. We live in a world that spins on the axel of belief. Now, what is your belief level? Do you believe? What do you believe for yourself? What greatness is hidden deep within you that only the key of belief will unlock? Listen to me. Blind people have been made to see. Deaf people have been made to hear. Sick people have been made whole again because they simply believed. They used the power of belief to heal their frail, sick bodies. They used the power of belief to set world records in running, swimming, and in sports. They used the power of belief to walk again. They used the power of belief to do what doctors and nurses told them would be impossible. Why? They believed. Do you believe? You must believe. It is your ticket to freedom. It is your ticket to success. It is your ticket to having everything in life that you've ever wanted, but you can't get it unless you believe! "I would have fainted, lest I believed," the Psalmist said.

You can't make it to where you're going on your own. You must believe, and you must have the power of belief working for you. You must decide to believe. You must choose belief. It's all about belief, and you don't develop belief by watching the news, TV, or playing golf. And you must know that your belief will make all the difference in the world.

# Chapter 9

# TWO GREAT ENEMIES
# OF SUCCESS

There are two great enemies of success. They are distractions and discouragement. Either one or both will keep you from achieving your dreams. The enemy of distraction is very deceitful because you can be involved in what's good, but be doing so at the expense of what's great. You chose being good over being great. That's a sad commentary. There are millions of things that can distract us. And what distracts me may or may not distract you. Sports consume some while others can't stand it. People have hobbies that can become a distraction if it's not put into perspective. Friends and unproductive relationships can be a powerful distraction. In fact, they have the power to ruin your resolve to be successful, or at least to not try as hard. They can tell you that you work too much or that you spend too much time working on your business or investing. They mean well. Their intentions are well founded, but you know what they say about good intentions. You can be sincere, and be sincerely wrong. Earnestness and sincerity do not validate good intentions. You must guard against time distractions. People can be time distractions. Friends that you should not have can be distractions. Sports can be a distraction. Your job can be a distraction. Your past successes can be a distraction. I hear this so many times from people who always talk about the one victory they had or the benchmarks they set way back when. They live in their past successes. They relish their trophies. Living in your past successes will distract and prevent you from claiming and striving for new ones. It's great and wonderful what you've done, but it can hold you back if you don't let them go. Celebrate your success and then move on. Don't become a legend in your own mind and in your own right. Let other men praise thee and not your own lips. Honor will be given where honor is due, but it is your job to keep moving, keep growing, and keep getting better.

Distractions will cause you to lose focus and as Mike Murdock stated and I quoted earlier, "The only reason men fail is broken focus." Distractions cause defeat. Distractions cause us to fail. Distractions bring about heartache. Distractions can make the dream foggy. Distractions can give you a false sense of security and reality. They are dangerous, and they are destructive. You must be constantly aware of the distractions that you allow in your life. That is why you must learn to say "no." That is why you can't make everyone happy all of the time. You must turn down what's good to continue pursuing your best. Realize that it is in your control to eliminate distractions and prevent new ones from coming into your life. Remember, wealth is not an accident. It won't just hit you on top of the head one day. You must not allow distractions to break your focus. Everyone and everybody, knowingly or unknowingly, consciously or unconsciously, will vie for your time, money, and attention never realizing that they are the very distractions that will keep you from attaining all that has been reserved for you. You must have a spirit of discernment to recognize between distractions and hindrances and what will be helpful and useful on your success journey. Just consciously being aware of distractions will help you make better decisions. Don't break your focus.

Discouragement has ruined more potential winners than any other single factor I know. It is easy to get discouraged and hard to get pumped back up again. Discouraged people don't win. Discouraged political candidates don't win elections. People don't go into business with discouraged business partners. People don't play on teams with discouraged players. Why? Discouragement is the cancer of any team, business, or organization. Discouragement will eat you up from the inside out. Discouragement, or disappointed goals, causes a deep level of frustration and depression. The good news is that you only get discouraged if you are a passionate person, otherwise you wouldn't care. The reason that's critical is because of the role that passion will play in your success. The level of passion with which you live life will have a direct effect on the kinds of people you attract to you, and remember, you are the same person today that you'll be five years from now except for the books you read and the people you meet. What will cause you to attract the people into your life that can make all the difference in the world for you? The difference is passion. The difference is that spark in your eye that makes you come alive with energy and enthusiasm and a zest for life.

People will spend millions of dollars to buy that feeling. We live in a world that craves and seeks after entertainment. We have the need to be entertained. We've created that never-ending, never-satisfied appetite in ourselves. People will pay more money to be entertained than they will to learn how to increase their wealth. They'll pay $20 at the movie theatre for one movie and then think twice before buying this book! They will eat out and never think twice about it. What they don't realize is that you can live without food, but you can't live without passion. People buy fancy cars and luxury houses with money they don't have, and they need to quit trying to impress themselves. They're leading lives of quiet desperation every month when the bills come in. They are buying things they don't need, with money they don't have, to impress people they don't like. The crumbs off a rich man's table are better than a feast with fools! Sharp isn't what you own, it's who you are and who you become. Yet people derive such a sense of self-worth from what car they drive and what neighborhood they live in and what country clubs they belong to. That doesn't make the man; that reveals the man. I was always told growing up that playing sports developed character. I believe that playing sports reveals your character as much as or more so than developing it. The only way it might be developing it is through the submission to authority, learning to play as a team (unselfishness), and being at practices and games on time and not quitting. However, we learn more from what we see than from what we hear. When we see our parents quitting jobs, quitting relationships, quitting marriages, quitting exercise programs, quitting their diets, what do we expect? When are we going to start looking in the mirror, accepting personal responsibility and saying that the problem starts here! That's how you beat discouragement. You take responsibility for what has happened, and you move forward. You don't stop, and you don't stand still. You get focused and make some changes to your own attitude and belief.

It's nobody's fault but your own if you stay discouraged. So something didn't go your way. Boo-hoo. So you were passed up for the promotion. So you didn't get the contract you were looking for. So your client or prospect decided to go somewhere else. So you lost some money. So you got the short end of the stick. So you were done wrong. MOVE ON!!! If you can't change it, then don't dwell on it. Think only of a solution. But discouragement will kill you. And the longer you allow yourself to be discouraged, the more dangerous it gets. It's kind of like the first time you threaten your spouse with divorce. It seems like the next several arguments always end up there. It's best if it never gets to that point to begin with. Discouragement is the main reason why people quit anything. Discouragement will keep you from making that next phone call. Discouragement will keep you from your next meeting. It will keep you from reading today. It will hinder you from thinking the way you need to and controlling your mind. Discouragement will rob you of your personal pride and sense of self-worth and will cause you to talk down to yourself. You can't be afraid to lose. You can't be afraid of defeat. You'll learn to walk when you get tired of falling down. But you have to guard and protect your thinking to prevent discouragement. Not hitting a specific goal can cause disappointment. I rarely change goals; however, I'm constantly changing the dates on those goals. I realize something of great priority along the way and adapt my plans and goals accordingly. But I don't let that get me discouraged. It doesn't mean I failed. I just didn't get it within the time frame I allotted. It's okay. As long as I've got breath in my body, then the game is not over. There's still time. I can still make it–if I do not get discouraged!

Hope deferred makes the heart sick. Discouragement over disappointed goals is natural. However, so is losing your temper, but that doesn't mean that it's a good thing to do! Defend yourself when you don't see a goal realized. Set new goals. Constantly be writing them down with new timelines based on the events that are going on. But don't allow discouragement to take up residency in your mind. The voice of

*Reflection on the Riches from this Chapter*

↪ The two great enemies of success are distractions and discouragement.

↪ Earnestness and sincerity do not validate good intentions.

↪ Your past successes can be a distraction.

↪ Discouragement has ruined more potential winners than any other single factor I know.

↪ You can live without food, but you can't live without passion.

↪ It's nobody's fault but your own if you stay discouraged.

↪ Discouragement is the main reason people quit anything.

↪ Don't allow discouragement to take up residency in your mind. The voice of discouragement is hard to keep quiet.

*Chapter 10*

# EYE OF THE TIGER

I s success optional to you? Will you be okay if you aren't successful? You may lack passion. You may lack the innate, but very detectable character trait of passion. Passion can give you favor with man. You will attract certain people into your life simply because of what you are passionate about. Likewise, you will drive some people from your life because of what you are passionate about. Passion creates momentum, and momentum is priceless. It cannot be bought. Momentum is like compounding interest; it can work for you or against you. But if you are on the right end of momentum, it will exponentially propel you to limits you didn't know existed. Passion is the mother of momentum. A life without passion is a life without hope. Passion is the seed by which success is born. Passion is the father of wealth.

How do you create that sense of urgency within yourself? How do you stir that ember and fan that flame that is within all of our bosoms? Passion, like belief, is a conscious choice. You become passionate about the things you devote your time, energy, and money to. The more passionate I am about a charity, church, or cause, the more I give. And the more I give, the more interested I am in that cause. I become more passionate about its success. So it is with you and me. Passion for people, passion for a business, passion for a product, or passion for winning is fueled by giving our time and money to it. The more time you spend with your family, the more passionate you will be about what happens to them. The more money you put into your investments and businesses, the more passionate you will become about them.

Passion controls your energy level. Passion can give you energy when it seems like you shouldn't have any. Passion can cause you to lose sleep at night. Passion can keep you up at night and wake you early in the morning. Passion can cause you to forget to eat and erase hunger pains. Trying to be successful without passion is like taking the bus instead of a jet. There is no comparison. Trying to achieve success without passion is to invite distractions, discouragement, and eventual failure into your life. You must live your life with relentless passion to experience the level of success that I want you to achieve. I am writing in one book what I had to read many books to learn and then compile. How do you put all of the success books together to become the nicest, wealthiest, healthiest, and happiest rich man that ever lived? That's what this book is intended to do for you.

I have done all the right things, gone to the right places, said the appropriate words, but doing everything right isn't always enough. Those things aren't enough. It takes passion. You can't touch it. You can't teach it. It's caught more than taught. But you know it's real. It's more real than most of what we call our reality. We know it exists like we know we exist. We know when we are living life with passion, and we know when we are living our life without it. And you certainly know the difference. You can also see different results from the times you were living with passion as compared to the times you weren't.

If your destiny is one of wealth, riches, and success, then you are commanded to live with passion. Be passionate about everything you do. Be passionate in your conversation and with everyone you talk to. Be passionate in your meetings and your daily activities at work. Be passionate about your family and marital relationships. Be passionate about everything you set your hand to do, and you will realize a level of success that few people ever experience because they came just short of selling all out and being passionate about the things that really mattered to them. They might hold back in part because they don't want to be considered "fanatical" about anything. I can tell you right now that if you aren't fanatical about success, you'll never taste it. You'll never know what it feels like to have more money than you know what to do with. You'll never live life the way you were born to experience it without passion.

Passion creates opportunities. Passion will open doors where they aren't any. Passion is your ticket to prosperity. Don't let anybody rob you of your passion. Some call them dream-stealers. Whatever you call them, they are out there. They are real. People will tell you that you are all talk. Once again, success is the sweetest revenge. When someone I respected told me that, I just dug my heels in and told myself, "I'll show you." I was stating what I wanted to happen in my life and his disbelief in my ability to do it ignited me with a fiery passion to prove to him that I wasn't all talk. What will it take to make you passionate? Will it take a tragedy? Will it take someone you love or respect telling you that you can't do it? Will it take losing your job to get passionate about your financial freedom? What will it take? I hope it doesn't take any of these things. I hope you learned from this chapter that you can't afford to live another day without a fiery passion driving you.

*Reflections on the Riches from this Chapter*

- Passion is the father of wealth and the mother of momentum.

- Passion creates opportunity.

- Trying to be successful without passion is like taking the bus instead of a jet–there's no comparison!

- Passion will give you energy when it seems like you shouldn't have any.

*Chapter 11*

# MONEY CAN'T THINK

One of the greatest lessons I learned that put wealth into perspective for me was that wealth didn't play favorites. A beautiful mansion doesn't decide that it will only let certain people live there. It doesn't control that. What determines where you get to live is the amount of money you have. The 2x4's don't say, "I like you, and I don't like you." They don't have wills, minds, or opinions. Cars don't say, "I like you. I will let you drive me." Material wealth can be had by anyone who has the money to pay for it. It doesn't have teacher pets. Even so, money doesn't mind who its owner is. That's what takes the mystery out of money. That's why you don't have to be deceitful or a crook to achieve significant monetary gain. You must simply find a need and fill it or find a better way of doing something. For example, find a way that I don't have to stop for gas every few days and you'll make a killing. Develop an international wireless internet system so I can utilize that medium from anywhere in the world. Find something consumers need or something that will simplify their lives, and you have a product. It's even better if you're the only place they can get it from!

I realized that it wasn't the car of my dreams that didn't want me to drive it, it was my lack of funds to pay that sticker price that caused me not to drive my dream car. That let me know that there was nothing personal that money had against me. That was not the reason I didn't have any. I didn't have any because of my limited financial intelligence and education that limited my ability to determine the quality of an investment. This was the reason for my lack along with my mentality and way of thinking. I was the reason I didn't have more. And I'm still the reason I don't have more than I have now. I must continually get better and develop myself. Material possessions can be a great tool when put in the right hands. They can be used to spend time with friends, to close business deals, to develop relationships, and to bless others.

Yachts, jets, coaches, luxury mansions around the world, spectacular vacations, and fancy automobiles can bring comfort to your life. I personally know that I was *Born to be Rich*. I was born to experience this life. I know that. But it is my responsibility to see that I live the life I was born to live. What were you born for? Do you know that riches and wealth are what you are destined for? Do you know that greatness will ebb out of you like an overflowing river? If you were *Born to be Rich,* and you know it or simply desire it, then you must have the correct view of the role riches play in society and in our lives. Riches have long equaled power.

Those with money have always received preferential treatment. They are typically treated with greater respect from society. Their opinions are valued more highly, and they are in a greater position to make a difference. Is this you? Am I describing your goal in life perfectly? Then I've got some fantastic news for you. You are getting ready to experience a level of living that less than 5% of people on this earth know anything about. It is the most thrilling of any roller coaster ride. It will teach you about human nature. It will teach you about people skills. It will teach you how to be a mentor and influence people. It will empower you to make a difference in our country and in our world. It will develop your mind, speaking ability, negotiation skills, and all the other resources that are coveted by those who never live the fruit of success. It is not for the faint in heart nor is it for those that hope. You can't just hope you are successful. You can't just hope to live your dream. You must know. You must believe. You must accept nothing less. You must be brave. You must be courageous in the face of your opposition. By the way, your opposition isn't your peers. You are not against those going the same direction you are. I used to be worried that all the successful people would own the best homes and drive the best cars before I could purchase them. But then I learned that there are more exotic woods, marble, granite, gold, silver, and all other building materials left unused that I could build something unlike anything on this planet.

Once I understood this, I started blessing those that had what I wanted. Every time I saw the vehicle I wanted, I would say a blessing for that person. I asked that they would be blessed financially and that they would flourish with prosperity. Every time I saw a mansion that I would love to own and live in, I asked that their riches would be increased and that they would enjoy the benefits of untold wealth. This respect towards wealth and those that had attracted it keeps me focused on who and what it is that I'm racing against. I'm not racing against anyone else. I don't have to get it first. I only have to run my race. I am my greatest critic and enemy. I hold myself back. I slow myself down by the baggage that I refuse to let go of. It's okay if someone else is running faster or slower than I am. I'm not in competition with them. That is the danger of comparing. Comparing yourself to others can cause you to be discouraged or motivated. It can cause you to feel bad about where you are or grateful for your accomplishments. Comparing yourself rarely moves you closer to your goal. You have to stay focused on running your race. If you are a runner, you know that it slows you down to keep turning around to see who's behind you. If you are significantly ahead, it can give you a false sense of security. If they are in front of you, it can make you discouraged. I always think of the workhorse in this situation. If you want a workhorse to perform at its optimum, then you have to put blinders on him. You do this so he'll stay focused on the row he's supposed to plow. You and I just need to put blinders on at times and run our best race and let the chips fall where they may.

If you are anything like I am, then you want success badly, don't you? You want it more than anything else. You want success so bad it affects every fiber of your body and consumes every waking thought of your day. I can remember nights that I would just sit out in the evening breeze or by the ocean and dream about the day that I would be living my dream. I would reflect many times on the weekends. I remember Saturday evenings always seemed to end in a time of great reflection. I would spend a lot of time in the bookstore. I would sit outside with a pen and paper and write my own dreams and goals one more time. I would write down different ways of achieving them. I would crunch numbers into the night. I would think about how I could go from where I was to where I wanted to be. One of the keys to accomplishing this was to be creative and flexible. I have been extremely creative in my methods of making money. Hardly anything I've done where I made large sums of money was done by traditional methods of making money. Being creative is extremely important when making business and investment decisions. But creativity alone isn't enough because a lot of times you have to be flexible. That's alright because your flexibility forces you to become even more creative to put business deals together and develop game plans to accomplish your mission. Flexibility and creativity in working with people is also extremely valuable. You are sure to experience smoother relationships and more profitable relationships by learning to increase your level of flexibility and determination to be more creative.

By having the right perspective about wealth and riches, you will be prepared to accept them graciously into your life. Wealth is not a right; it's a privilege that is earned. It is safe and secured only by a positive mentality and a right attitude and thought life concerning it. The right way of thinking is the greatest insurance you will ever have to protect your number one asset. You must have this thought life toward riches in order to attract them into your life.

*Reflections on the Riches from this Chapter*

- Wealth doesn't play favorites.

- Your enemy is not those going the same direction you are.

- Comparing yourself to others rarely moves you closer to your goal.

- Hardly anything you do where you make large sums of money will be done without creativity.

- Wealth is not a right; it's a privilege that is earned.

- Wealth is only secured and insured by a positive mentality and right attitude.

*Chapter 12*

# CONSISTENCY MATTERS

If you were *Born to be Rich,* then you have already learned or will soon be learning the role that consistency will play in your success.

Consistency is a lost art in our world today. Inconsistency is all around us. People say one thing and do another. They run hard for a little while and then they back off. They are motivated one month and not the next. They discipline their children this time, but they let it slide the next. They sprint through life, and then they coast. They sprint, then coast—sprint, then coast. People are inconsistent in their beliefs. They say they believe many things are more important than money such as family, God, friends, etc. However, their actions contradict their inconsistent "belief," or what they think they believe. A true belief is followed by action, but most people's inconsistent "belief" structure is not followed by the actions that would be consistent of that belief. This creates instability in mankind. It causes emotional problems and turmoil and can give false illusions of reality thus impairing your judgment and decision-making abilities. If family was more important than money to them, then they would spend more time with their family and less time trading time for dollars on a job. If a good marriage was really more important than money, then they would treat their spouse with the same level of respect, and preferably more, than they do their boss. They aren't always nitpicking their boss (to their face). They aren't always cutting down the boss and telling him he isn't worth spit. God doesn't make junk. Yet we treat those that we say are more important to us than anything in this world like their mere existence is an irreversible fallacy. How sad!

We are inconsistent in our thinking. This creates chaos and a double-minded man. The Word says that a "double-minded man is unstable in all his ways." Inconsistency impairs your discernment when making decisions. Consistent effort combined with consistent actions, mixed with consistent right thinking, and blended with a consistent positive belief structure will inevitably and systematically breed success. Even if you are just consistent with increasing your own business, success, and wealth education, you will attract the people and the books required to lead you toward the destiny for which you were born.

People aren't consistent with their health. Every year, New Year's resolutions are made and broken within a mere six weeks. People do not remain consistent. Once again, people become inconsistent when they lose their focus. They lose sight of the reason they are doing what they are doing. They lose the value that they once had placed on that particular activity. Now this is necessary at times in life to prioritize your schedule and goals. The problem isn't that people don't have enough time; it's that they don't know how to prioritize their time.

To become fabulously wealthy, you must learn to be consistent in your life. You must consistently be a student of people. People are the only things in this world that have money. The more consistent you are about learning about people, the more money you will make. Nobody will ever be as concerned about your financial situation as you are. It is your responsibility to be consistent. You must invest consistently. You must save consistently. You must be consistent with guarding your time. You must consistently eat right. You must exercise consistently to reap the benefits and the rewards. Everybody has things they want to do, but most people are doing things they have to do. Why? They have not learned to find the right investments or businesses and consistently invest the necessary time and money in them so that their money will work for them. The average person gets frustrated with their job seven times a year, yet they don't do anything about it! This inconsistent pattern in their thinking will drown them in a sea of annual frustration lest they learn to consistently take action that will change their situation. I heard Mark Victor Hansen once say, "You should work forty hours to survive, and work forty hours to move on." That's good advice. That eliminates the fear of just quitting your job and starting a business and all the sudden being an expert real estate and stock market professional. But too many people have joined the Who's Who book of "Who's Finished in America!" Don't let this be your commentary. You don't belong on that list if you were *Born to be Rich*. The biggest oxy-moron I've ever heard in the professional world is that someone has a "good job." I don't care what age you are, it's not too late to learn and implement these principles in your life. The only thing worse than being broke at fifty-five is being broke at sixty-five. It takes an enormous amount of discipline to be consistent, but the pain of discipline is temporary; the pain of regret is permanent. Our discipline determines our habits; our habits determine our destiny. And as Les Brown said, "It's not over until you win!" Discipline must come from within or it will be imposed from

*Reflections on the Riches from this Chapter*

- Consistency is a lost art.

- Inconsistency impairs your discernment when making decisions.

- The only thing worse than being broke at fifty-five is being broke at sixty-five.

- The pain of discipline is temporary; the pain of regret is permanent.

- Discipline must come from within or it will be imposed from without.

- Adversity is your friend, and complacency is your enemy.

# Chapter 13

# ACCOUNTABILITY
# ISN'T AN OPTION

Be accountable to someone. Be accountable for your activity. Be accountable to someone for your finances. Be accountable to someone for your marriage. Be accountable to someone for your business. Hold yourself accountable by allowing yourself to be accountable to someone else. You must be dream-oriented, but stay purpose-focused. Accountability will help you stay the course. Besides, there are only two ways to learn. The first is by a mentor and the second is by mistakes. The first is faster, cheaper, and more fun!

Mentors will stick with you when you're going through the rough times that you inevitably must go through. Rats will flee a sinking ship, but sailors will plug the holes. That's what a mentor will do for you. They will plug the holes that are causing your ship to sink. They provide buoyancy to keep the ship afloat by the sound wisdom and advice for your specific situation. You must be willing to invest the time to be accountable to someone. Know your own worth so that you don't need constant reassurance. I received an email from one of my mentors one time that went like this:

A well-known speaker started off his seminar by holding up a $20 bill. In the room of 200, he asked, "Who would like this $20 bill?" Hands started going up all over the room. The speaker said, "I am going to give this to one of you, but first, let me do this." He proceeded to crumple the bill up. He then asked the crowd, "Who still wants it?" Hands were still up in the air. "Well," he replied, "What if I do this?" He dropped it on the ground and started to grind it into the floor with his shoe. He picked it up and said, "Now who wants it?" Still, hands went into the air.

"My friends, you all have learned a valuable lesson. No matter what I did to the money, you still wanted it because it did not decrease in value. It was still worth $20 dollars. Many times in our lives, we are dropped, crumpled, and ground into the dirt by the decisions we make and the circumstances that come our way. We feel that we are worthless, but no matter what happened or what will happen, you will never lose your value, dirty or clean, crumpled or finely creased; you are still priceless to those who love you. The worth of our lives comes not in what we do or who we know, but by who we are. You are special. Don't ever forget it!"

A mentor will help you concentrate your vision on the long-term good rather than the quick fix. Think about the big things while you're doing the little things to stay focused. Long-term frustration is insanity, and you must protect your focus with the help of wise counsel to prevent this.

Accountability is a leadership fundamental. Good leaders set expectations and then hold themselves and others accountable for their actions. Expectation management, followed by consistent accountability, prevents favoritism from occurring. It eliminates one person receiving preferential treatment above another because all are being held accountable to the same expectation. You should hold yourself to a higher standard than your boss could ever legally hold you too. I expect more out of myself than anyone else ever could. Hold yourself accountable for attaining excellence in every area of your life. Don't settle for mediocrity. Don't tolerate average if excellence is the standard.

Many people set standards and resolutions. Few people exceed their standards or fulfill their resolutions due to lack of accountability. Where does the problem lie? The area of opportunity is found on the doorstop of accountability. Why don't more people hold themselves accountable? It takes discipline. Society has made it acceptable to be undisciplined in the name of creativity and individuality. Lack of personal discipline is the primary driver leading to poor levels of accountability. People have been blaming others for their problems and plot in life for so long that it would be an uphill battle to recondition them to take personal responsibility for their life's state. Accountability begins with a person taking personal responsibility for where they are and who they are. How can a person of integrity hope to hold others accountable when they are woefully inadequate at holding themselves accountable? They cannot. Leaders must be true to themselves and to others.

Many people are reluctant to be accountable to someone else for fear of failure. They want and need their mentor to be proud of them. For their mentor to see anything but success emit from them translates into failure in their mind. If you have a true mentor that is focused on your success, then that is the furthest thing from the truth. They are not basing the continuation of mentorship on the number of wins and losses you have. If you fear "losing face" with your mentor, I recommend you openly discuss that fear with them or find a new one. While it is natural to want to "save face" with other people, it should not be a concern with your mentor. For a mentor to be effective in your life, you must be comfortable with them. It is natural to want to please them by achieving success as that is their "reward" for their long hours invested into you.

Accountability to yourself and others is a necessary component of achieving the wealth you desire. You will be accountable to your spouse, your employees, the IRS, and governing bodies. There may be many more people you are accountable to. Don't dread accountability. Realize that it is the glue that holds you together during the storms of life. When the dark clouds seem to linger, accountability ensures you continue the behaviors that will see you through to the other side. No problem lingers forever. The seasons of life bring good times and bad times. You won't always be in the valley, nor will you always reside on the mountain tops. The sun will not always shine, but the rain is not permanent either! Without the rain, the sun would not seem special. Without the bad times, you would not be able to recognize or be grateful for the good times. If you did not know what a valley looked like, then you would not see the mountain top. Let accountability be the stabilizer that sees you through the bumps as you travel Success Lane.

*Reflections on the Riches from this Chapter*

- Hold yourself accountable by being accountable to someone else.

- Rats (pseudo-friends) will flee a sinking ship, but sailors (mentors) will plug the holes.

- Know your own worth so that you don't need constant reassurance from those around you.

- Concentrate your vision on the long-term good rather than the quick fix.

- Think about the big picture while you're doing the little things to stay focused.

# Chapter 14

# RESULTS OF A POWERFUL IMAGE

Projecting a powerful image is vital to achieving success. Perceived strength, wisdom, and leadership can scale you up the highest mountains of success, and perceived weakness in these areas can bury you deeper than the deepest ocean. Your image determines whether you get the job or lose the job, get the client, prospect, or contract, or fail to close the transaction. Conveying a powerful image is essential to your wealth and success. However, in order to convey that perception, you must know who you really are. And if you don't become the same thing you project, you won't know who you are.

Nobody likes a hypocrite. Nobody likes people who pretend to be something they are not. No one likes people who try to sound smarter than they are or act wealthier than they are. It is a big turn-off. No one likes a copycat. People don't like imitators. They don't need a miniature somebody else. This world needs you to be you. You were placed here because of who you are and what you have to share, so don't copy those that you emulate. There are success habits that everyone should copy. I'm talking about being an exact replica and losing your own self-identity. I've heard speakers that try to talk like other speakers. I've read books where the author wanted to be like someone else. You have to be you. The only way to successfully project a powerful image is to BE the image that you convey. You must be a learned individual from reading books and evaluating the markets and other people. This knowledge is not found in any academic institution anywhere. It is learned from books and mentors. This is not a subject that very many people talk about, but it is a foundation to all of our success. We didn't talk like we were weak, pathetic, sickly, inferior creatures to those that were in a position of power to help us or hire us. We didn't cower down and act like they were better than us. We didn't wimp out and let fear get the best of us. We didn't just say what we thought they wanted to hear. We shot straight with tact. Remember that phrase–shoot straight with tack. That will be a major element that will alleviate many problems for you. Don't sugar-coat, but don't beat them over the head. Don't go around the barn or beat around the bush, but don't run a tractor-trailer through it either. Always put yourself in the other person's mind and speak ahead of their thoughts. If you know what they are going to say, form your words to effectively remove any objections or negative responses. This is part of your image. You must practice this skill until it becomes second nature. Have you ever noticed that when your mentor comes into the room, everybody looks at him/ her? Have you ever noticed the respect that certain people command just because of the way they carry themselves? The powerful image that they convey commands respect. It is possible for people to become overly confident and tread into the greatly disliked group of those we call "cocky." You want to make sure that you know the difference and avoid the latter at all cost. Nobody likes people who do nothing but brag about themselves. People like to be bragged on, but they don't like to hear you brag on yourself. Most people already know what you have accomplished and don't need you to remind them of "who you are" every time you are around them.

To project your most powerful image is not to walk around like others are beneath you. You will be very friendly and kind. Nevertheless, because of all the work you have done developing yourself, others can sense a difference in your mentality and attitude based on your projected image. The key to successfully transmitting these vibes is for them to flow through you naturally by becoming the person you are projecting. Inconsistency in this area will cause the opposite reaction from people, and they will be skeptical of you. Have you ever said, "You know, I don't know what it is about that person, but I don't like or trust them." It is probably because they were trying to project an image that was inconsistent with who they really are.

That brings us to the next thought. You attract who you are, not who you want. So many managers get upset that they can't find good help—people who aren't lazy, who can close a sale, or who can develop relationships with clients. What they don't realize is that they attract who they are. They have to change and miraculously, they will start attracting a better quality employee. When I was an employee seeking work, I remember eliminating possible jobs because I refused to work for certain managers. I could tell that they were going nowhere, and I did not believe in their leadership ability. I did not feel like there was anything I could learn from them that would take me closer to my goal of being free. I've been offered several jobs and continue to receive occasional offers. Several I would not accept simply because of the person that owned the business or the management of the firm. They failed to successfully recruit me, not because of the pay, benefits, or the actual job. They failed to recruit me because of who they were, and they will probably never admit that to themselves so that they can move on and do something about it. If they would read more books on success, business, sales, closing, personal finances, self-development, people skills, and start attending success seminars and hanging around people who have already been where they're at, I would probably consider the offer with more than a casual glance.

Projecting a powerful self-image will get you business that you would not have otherwise received. A powerful image will lead you to the people who can make things happen for you. I believe this with all of my heart. I appreciate what Mike Murdock once said, "One day of favor is worth a thousand days of labor." One day of favor from the right person can open doors to you that all the wealth in the world could not have opened, yet you will be invited in and propelled to the level of greatness you were born to live.

You must be bold. You must not shy away from problems, but rather address them quickly and confidently. You can't procrastinate in handling problems. This will cause a lack of respect to develop among those who look to you for leadership. Finally, realize that a powerful image doesn't just happen. It isn't something you put on in the morning. A thousand dollar suit doesn't cover up stupidity or ignorance. It is very important what you wear; don't get me wrong. But realize that clothes don't make the man, contrary to what the ads tell you. Clothes can certainly enhance and add a wonderful, vibrant aura of success if adorned properly and tastefully. The important thing to never, ever forget is that a powerful image isn't what you wear; it's who you are.

## Reflections on the Riches from this Chapter

- Projecting a powerful image is vital to achieving success.

- Shoot straight with tact.

- The key to projecting a powerful image is to be the person you are projecting.

- You attract who you are, not what you want.

- You can't procrastinate in handling problems.

- A powerful image isn't what you wear; it's who you are.

*Chapter 15*

# THE ART OF INFLUENCE

There's no doubt that earners are learners. Not all learners are earners, however. Maybe that isn't why they were born. Perhaps they aren't learning the necessary things to earn. Some people try to know a little bit about everything and become a jack-of-all-trades and a master-of-none.

However, there is one topic that to achieve great wealth, you cannot afford to casually learn. It must consume you, and you must become a master at it. Your success will be predicated in proportion to the degree to which you master the art of working with people. When you realize that you can start arguments, stop arguments, raise self esteem, lower self esteem, close a sale, or lose the customer forever, you will understand the importance of greater people skills. You have the power to make people say "Yes." You have the power to turn horrible situations into productive ones. You have the power to restore relationships. You also have the power to prevent relationships from being ruined. Your success is on life support and you've got the cord in your hand right now. What you say next will either keep it plugged in or yank it out of the wall.

We all know that people are different. But if we look at

people generically and as a whole, we realize that people are not all that different. History repeats itself because people keep making the same mistakes. People keep making the same mistakes because they didn't learn from their previous ones, much less the mistakes of others. But people keep making the same mistakes also because they fail to study people. They don't understand what makes someone tick. They don't know what makes somebody fly off the handle. Have you ever heard someone say, "Did what I say bother you?" or "Was it something I said?"

I have spent a fair amount of my professional career interviewing potential managers and employees. I would say that no less than 97% of the people I interview tell me that one of their strong points is their people skills. I have had people that couldn't look me in the eye tell me that. I have had people who couldn't carry on a conversation with me about the weather, sports, or anything else, tell me that they had great people skills. This area has become so clouded and muddied over the past decade that I got to where I dreaded hearing someone say that their people skills are one of their strengths. Whether or not you have people skills is a personal opinion. I could think you have great people skills and someone else could think that you lack them greatly. One reason for this discrepancy is that people fail to relate to other people. I believe that is what people skills really are—the ability to relate to other people.

If you can't relate to every single person you ever meet and be able to pull the best out of them and know right away what makes them tick, what motivates them, what scares them, what turns them off, what excites them, what confuses them, and what causes them to perform at their highest and best use, then you don't have the people skills that you need.

There are times that I have chosen not to relate to someone. When you have people skills, you leave people feeling better about themselves from when you found them. I remember my mentor telling me that people only remember you by how they felt after being in your presence. How did they feel when you left? Were they empowered? Were they motivated to action? Were they challenged, perhaps without words, to be more enthusiastic and passionate? How do you leave people feeling about themselves?

To master people skills, you must understand the different personalities. I'm not going to address in a chapter what mountains of books have covered. I will simply direct you to the one that I am going to reference and the one that I adhere to. It is the easiest one for me to remember. I use Dr. Robert Rohm's *Positive Personality Profiles*. He uses the D.I.S.C. system. Other people use the conventional method: choleric, sanguine, melancholy, and phlegmatic. Still others use the ancient Chinese animal system which includes the lion, otter, golden retriever, and beaver. Regardless of the system that is easiest for you to remember, they all have the same four main personality types. Some people might have a little bit of both, but one usually prevails. The first type of person is the go-getter. This is the guy that is a hard-charger. He's oftentimes like a bull in a China shop. He never quits. He will plow over people and not care about them or what they think. He is a visionary; management and leadership come naturally for him. Now, not all the people that fit in this category exemplify all of these traits. They might have developed themselves to the place that they no longer exhibit the poor attributes that are natural for them. That's the goal.

The next type of person is very outgoing. They are loud. They are fun to be around and are the life of the party. If people aren't having fun, they will single-handedly turn it around. They have high highs and low lows. They are easily motivated and excitable, but when they hit the bottom, it's rock bottom. They aren't sure they can go on. They don't know if life's worth living. They are very emotional people, and they must be handled with care. The good thing about these people is that if you say something that hurts or offends them, you can usually apologize, and that will be the end of it. They don't like for there to be tension among people. They like for everybody to get along and work together.

The next person is usually reserved. They aren't shy around the people they know, but people they don't know will think that they are shy or snobs. You know they are not shy because of the way they act in front of their friends. These people are usually very supportive of their friends, family, and co-workers. They are very understanding, good-natured, and loving people. They will be extremely loyal to you if you treat them right. Even if they have an opinion or preference, they will generally keep it to themselves. They want to please the people they're around. They avoid conflict and confrontation at all cost. They are generally flexible, easy-going people.

The last type of individual is the person that thinks analytically. They are very methodical in their lives. They don't like change. They are typically very organized people who can appear reserved, but won't budge on an opinion or belief they have because they have fully analyzed all the possibilities and have drawn their own conclusions. They are very calculating and smart. They show very little, if any, emotion. They will listen to what you have to say, and their response will be broken down to you in outline form beginning with Roman numeral I.

So how do we put a lot of people in the same area with

these personality types and expect them to get along. Well, many don't because they don't understand that everyone is born with an inclination to one of these personalities. People can change. They cannot be so harsh and less demanding, and they cannot have such high highs and low lows by controlling their emotions. They can speak up every now and then and give their opinion to join the conversation, and they can show an emotion every now and then. They don't have to remain the way they are just because "that's their personality." But whether anyone ever changes or not doesn't really matter. You are still able to accomplish your goals and dreams as long as you know how to get all of the different personalities to see things your way and to get them on your team and make them feel loved.

Understanding this will raise your sales. Understanding and utilizing this information will make you a much better husband or wife. Practicing this method will cause you to bring people together and successfully cause them to be productive because you know what to say to whom, when to say it, and how to say it. I'm sure you were told as a child that it's not what you say as much as it is how you say it.

For example, I could tell my wife in a questioning tone, "That's a pretty dress?" Or I can say the exact same words with warmth, love, and a hint of seduction, "Thaaaat's a pretty dress!" I just went from being a villain to Don Juan! I said the exact same words, but my tone would have caused me to hurt her with the first way I said it. The second way would have resulted in a kiss. It's important that you think about how you say things before you say it. Of course, it's important to think about what you are going to say before you open your mouth as well. Now, suppose that everything I'm saying to a prospective client, I'm going up on the end of my sentences. That's a questioning tone. When you ask a question, you generally go up on the end of the question. Ask out loud right now, "Do you want to go shopping?" See what I mean? Okay, so I'm talking to my prospective client, and I'm using that questioning tone: "Would you be interested in hearing more about our service?" He believes that I'm unsure of my product or that my belief in my proposition is wavering. He will have that feeling that he's not quite sure, but he doesn't think it's the right timing to buy. He can also sense that I do not expect him to answer in the affirmative. And what just happened was that the way you said your presentation caused him to question and to doubt the validity of your product or proposal. Practice going down on the end of your sentences or at least straight across (but not monotone). You can teach yourself this skill just by practicing.

If you can't tell by now, I am an achiever. I'm a driver. I am success-oriented and drawn to management and leadership. But let's say that I'm around someone else with the same personality as mine that does not understand themselves, much less anybody else. How do I act in that situation? Would we not go head-to-head? Would there not be strife and a power struggle? Not on your life. If I want that person to like me and to work hard for me, I will give them perceived power, but I'm the one giving it to them; therefore, I am in control of that person. I draw the line on how far they are able to go. I don't tell them that; I use tact. I might say something in a group setting that is meant for that one person or those personalities. If I said it directly to them, it would start a fight. But by using the power of suggestion, I am able to ask the right questions that will lead them to the conclusion that I have come up with for them. This is not manipulation; it is knowing people and exercising good people skills. What I am teaching you is not a tactic, it is a philosophy. This is called getting along with others. This is what you were supposed to do on the playground and in the sandbox. If you are the one that grants me power, then you must have more power than I have. That's how I can control go-getters without them knowing or feeling controlled. It's a beautiful thing. Now let's say that I wanted to get another person with this personality to go to a success seminar. Now I know I'm probably going to hear, "I don't need all the motivation stuff. I'm already motivated, can't you tell? Those seminars are for people who aren't going anywhere in life." So I don't just ask, "Do you want to go to a seminar with me?" If I asked that, I would likely hear what I just said I didn't want to hear. But if I said, "Hey, I'm going to a success seminar, and there will be a lot of other leaders there. I want you to go with me so they can see your leadership." He's going to be there. I would further seal it by saying, "Anybody who's anybody will be there. All the leaders will be there." Then he is definitely going because he considers himself to be a leader.

What if I'm the leader type and I'm trying to get the life of the party person to go with me to a success seminar? Of course I get tired of his mood swings. Yes, he bugs me. But I have to learn how to work with him and motivate him if I want him to be able to help me achieve my goals. Now, he's looking back at me thinking that he'd never want to be as focused as I am because in his mind, that's not fun! He doesn't want to feel the pressure that I place on myself. He likes being happy-go-lucky. So I'm trying to get him to go with me to the success conference. All I really have to say to him is, "We're going to have a blast. It's going to be like one big party. It will be so much fun! A lot of friends will be there, and we will all go out to eat!" He will be all over it.

If I am going to get the person that prefers to stay out of the spotlight, has a great personality, but is only outgoing around their friends to a success seminar, I have to approach it differently than the first two personalities. I might say something to the effect of, "I'm going to a success seminar, and it would really mean a lot to me if you would go with me." They can't say "no." It's impossible for them because they don't like to disappoint others.

Now for Mr. Smarty-Pants, or Mr. Always Right, or Mr. Analytical (just letting my "D" personality out of the cage for a second!). I want this person that evaluates every little statement I make and every little detail (normally at the expense of the big picture) to go to a success seminar with me. I will say to them, "I'm going to a success seminar on such and such date and from such and such time, and I would like to invite you to go with me. The speakers will be speaking on XYZ topic, and they will have seventeen points with ten alliterated sub-points under each. Your hand will ache from the amount of quality information presented there. It is a seminar for serious professionals only." He's going to love it. He has just found his home. He will check his BlackBerry and say, "I am scheduling it right now."

I just took my personality to show how I would relate it to all four, including my own. I will not take the time to go through each personality and show how I would exercise people skills to accomplish that goal using each personality. I want you to do that. Pretend it is a game. The next person you meet, determine which one of these categories they fall in. Once you are able to start recognizing them, you will know exactly how to deal with each one.

Another important component to people skills is learning to mirror the person you are talking with. I do this on the phone and in daily conversation. I pride myself on adapting to them and not making them adapt to me. Why do I do that? I want them to be comfortable. I'm the expert at working and developing people. When people are comfortable, it is easier for them to speak the exact truth so you can find out what triggers to use. When I mirror another person, it puts them at ease. They let their guard down a little bit, and they lower their shield. This allows me to build a trust relationship with them. This is key if you are going to work with them. If they cross their legs, I'm going to cross mine. If they fold their arms and lean back all serious-like, then I'm going to do the same. If they speak slowly, then I will as well. If I speak fast to a person that speaks slowly, they will not trust me. They will think that I'm trying to pull the wool over their eyes. If they talk like they are in a hurry, then I talk like I am in a hurry. Does mirroring mean that I'm not leading? Quite the contrary, it means that you are leading them to the place that you are trying to get them to.

Learning to effectively mirror someone also means maintaining eye contact. You must maintain eye contact. However, some people feel very uncomfortable if you hold the eye contact for long stretches at a time. Don't bore holes in people. If they have trouble keeping eye contact with you, then they might be embarrassed or shy or feel inferior, and if you just stare at them regardless, they will feel uncomfortable. They will think that you can see right through them. It will also be easier for them to make a decision if you aren't staring at them because they will be more at ease. With that being said, the majority of the time, you will need to keep eye contact. If you don't, and you are talking to someone that does maintain eye contact, then they will not trust what you are saying. This is vitally important in business, politics, sales, and sports. You have to learn to put other people at ease by mirroring them.

If you master these principles, then you will be able to get a raise whenever you want because you know how to approach the boss. You know how to phrase and tone the request to get the answer you wish depending on which personality they have. Isn't that wonderful? I'm telling you that you will grow your business larger than you ever dreamed, cash and deposit checks larger than you imagined, and your praises will be sung once you are successful at implementing these golden rules of people skills. This is how you successfully get to the top without stomping on everybody else and using them as a ladder. People will feel good about your success. They will be proud to know you. They will want to work harder for you. They will see the diligence and wisdom and tact by which you conduct yourself. This information along with consistency, the right belief, the right thinking, and a powerful image will set you up for wealth and riches to flood into your life. You will begin to attract what once seemed to elude you. Reading it isn't enough. It must be practiced and mastered. You can't afford not to, and you will never achieve what you want to accomplish without this. I can promise you that. You will short-change your success by cheating if you fail to fully comprehend and utilize the power of working with people by relating to them.

*Reflection on the Riches from this Chapter*

- History repeats itself because people keep making the same mistakes.

- People skills are the skills needed to relate to other people.

- People only remember you by how they felt after being in your presence.

- People can change.

- You do not have to be your personality.

- Practice going down on the end of your sentences to avoid a questioning tone.

- Developing people skills is not a tactic, it is a philosophy.

- Mirror the person you are talking to in person or on the phone.

# Chapter 16

# DON'T CATCH THE ROTTEN TOMATOES

As you start to edge out from the average person, you will begin getting criticized. I heard as a boy that if you don't want to be criticized, then be nothing, do nothing, and say nothing, and no one will criticize you because most people, out of respect, don't criticize the dead! This is true. Any change you ever make in you, your business, company, or organization to better it, bring more accountability, or alter other's routines will be met with opposition and criticism. You can't throw a pebble or rock of any size into the water without causing some ripples. People will complain about this and that. They might even get testy at times. They will most certainly provide resistance to change. People resist change. That's why they won't work on themselves because they don't want to change, which is why they are exactly where they are. Mike Murdock has said, "If you want something you have never had, you have to do something you have never done." And that requires change. Look at all the zoning ordinances and meetings that are held to change them. I've seen entire cities come out to block a zoning change. They don't want their community to change. They don't want a huge shopping complex in their back yard. They don't want an apartment complex next door. They like their little town or city just the way it is, and if it never progressed, they would just sit back and be content. Unfortunately, that won't happen because there are too many people out there to allow life to just happen without keeping pace. I'm not satisfied with just keeping pace. I want to be a trend-setter. And if I'm to stick my neck and ideas out there, they are going to get swatted at from time to time. My mentor once said that the taller you stand out, the more tomatoes you catch in the face. Back when you were average, you didn't catch too many tomatoes. But as you started growing and developing and getting better, all the sudden, your co-workers started making fun of you. They didn't do that when you were one of them. They didn't make fun of you or criticize you when you were the same height as they were. But as you grew in your personal development and became head and shoulders above them, watch out. The tomatoes start flying. And one will catch you with your mouth open from time to time. Be prepared. I didn't say don't do it or run from it. I just said to be prepared. Be ready so that it doesn't take you by surprise. Be ready so you don't stumble around and fumble for a comeback. Know exactly where you stand and who you are. Take comfort in knowing where you are going.

One of the things that kept me going was knowing that one day I would say one of two things. I would either say, "I'm glad I did" or "I wish I had." I want to be able to say that I'm glad I did. I don't want to regret not going for my goals and dreams because I was more concerned with what my friends thought than my own destiny. I don't want to regret that I didn't go for my dreams because I didn't want people to talk bad about me or criticize me. I would hate to think that fear of what other people would say and think froze me into a state of complacency. Start today to have a new ending.

Criticism is one of those little things that make a big difference in the accomplishments of your dreams. Termites cause more damage each year than hurricanes and tornadoes combined. It is the little things that will bring you down if you don't watch out. Don't run from it, but understand the source. If you understand people from the previous chapter, it will enable you to better handle criticism. Just remember why you are doing what you are doing. This business of helping people is the highest calling one can have. Remember Who it is that you answer to.

*Reflections on the Riches from this Chapter*

🖎   You can't make a change without causing ripples.

🖎   People resist change.

🖎   If you want something you've never had, you must do something you've never done.     –Mike Murdock

🖎   Take comfort in knowing where you are going.

🖎   You will either say, "I'm glad I did" or "I wish I had."

*Chapter 17*

# WEALTH 101

If you were *Born to be Rich*, then you must learn to leverage both time and money. This was the hardest and most frustrating thing for me to understand. I could change my thinking, my belief, and how I worked with people, but this lesson was difficult for me to learn. That is why I'm such a fan of the Rich Dad series and, in particular, the CashFlow games. From playing those games, it gave us the framework and working knowledge we needed to ask our advisors and mentors the right questions to get the answers we needed to move forward.

To be rich, and I classify a rich person as a person with $10 million dollars in liquid capital or assets, you must leverage your time. You cannot do this if the forty best hours of your week are spent working for someone else. Your goal should be to start, build, or own assets that do not require your time or presence to make money. When I first started out in real estate, I owned over ten rentals including four-plexes, duplexes, and single family homes. It required very little time. My current real estate holdings require around twenty minutes a month of my time. These are the kind of assets that I look for. One of the businesses that I own today, I spend less than an hour a month working it, yet it produces positive monthly cash flow. That's the goal. The goal is to leverage your time. Find assets and businesses that can make money for you while you're sleeping. You must have a system for making money. If your system goes to sleep at night, then you don't have a system. That is, if you are the system, then you need to find a system that works for you twenty-four hours a day, 365 days a year. You won't achieve the compounding returns that you are yearning to earn if you don't understand that you cannot work hard enough or long enough to get as rich as you want to be. You will burn out before you rust out with that approach, and I don't want to do either one! I have written the majority of this book while sitting by the pool, gazing at the water, and the magnificent palm trees, and luxurious landscaping by which I'm surrounded. This isn't work to me, and I'm certainly not doing it for the money. I could probably get a high paying job and make more money in a year from it than in five years from the royalties of this book. I'm writing it to educate and inspire. My purpose in life is to inspire those that choose to be inspired to attain in every aspect of their lives: physically, mentally, spiritually, emotionally, socially, and financially to better themselves and the lives of those around them. That is my mission. If I'm to be rich, then I must fulfill my mission, and the money will come. But I can't just sit on the sidelines. I invest in my education, and then I invest. You must find businesses and investments that require a minimal amount of your time. Your income needs to be passive and residual.

Think about this. If your goal is to make $10,000 per month without a job and each of the assets you currently have make you $500 per month, and you have to work fifteen hours a week to achieve that $500, then to make $10,000 per month with similar assets yielding similar returns on your time investment, you need to buy twenty more investments like the one you have now. That means you will need to work 300 hours each week! That's a problem because there are only 168 hours in a week. What I'm trying to show you is that if your plan is similar to this, then you are spinning plates. You will not be able to reach your goal at your current pace. You must learn to find and buy investments and businesses that you can get a better return on your time. We talk so much about what percentage your money returns to you, but the simple truth is that if you can't realize that return with a minimal time investment, then you are going to be worn out and tired and eventually, you will just go back to a job because you at least get the weekends off and health insurance.

To be rich, you must not only leverage your time, you must do so while leveraging your money. An investment that you spend thirty minutes a month in that yields less than 5% won't cut it. On the other hand, an investment that you spend 100 hours in a month that yields 20% return may not be worth it either. It depends on the principle amount that's reaping the 20%. I would spend twenty-five hours a week in a business that netted me $10 million dollars per month. I would duplicate myself in somebody else, pay them $500,000 a year, and have them run the business. It's all relative, and that's why investing isn't black and white. That's why some people lose money and others make money.

You must leverage your money. Sure you can wait for thirty years to save a million dollars, but this book is not for you if that's your plan. You are more than welcome and entitled to do so. However, I didn't want to work that long and hard. I make more money in a month than I used to make in salary! I'm telling you that if you want to be rich, you must learn to leverage your money. It's the only way to grow time. Time can be manipulated and fast-forwarded if you use the power of leverage. If I only have $1000 to invest, then it's going to take me a long time to have $100,000 to invest. However, if I leverage my thousand dollars in a business or real estate, then it is likely that I can turn that $1000 into $10,000 and the $10,000 into $50,000, and that $50,000 into $200,000 within a few years. It is possible with the right financial education and investment vehicles. But the golden rule that you need to judge an investment by is not just the return on your cash investment but on your time investment as well. It may not be worth it. I can't tell you how many investments the numbers worked on, but what it would do to my schedule and my time shrinks the return down significantly.

Every employee that has more month than money does that right now. They don't calculate the amount of hours they work and compare their return on their time investment. I can hear the victim in this situation crying right now, "But what am I supposed to do? How can I get out of this? You're right. I make a great salary, but with the amount of hours I put in, I'm making minimum wage!" Fortunately for you the title of this book is not *Born to be Poor* but *Born to be Rich!*

For the investor starting out, it is in your best interest to keep your job and start a business on the side. You will need to spend some time getting it up and going, but you better duplicate yourself as soon as possible. Your goal should be to work yourself out of your job even if you own the business. You do this to free up your time to start or pursue the next asset. Leverage your time and money. You also need to seek competent tax and legal council to combine the strategies that are out there to maximize your net profits. I recently had lunch with my attorney, and she was talking about business owners who spend more time running their business than if they had a job. She said that most were making less money than they would at a job. That is not the kind of freedom I'm looking for! Most small businesses are started and operated by their owner. To be rich, you must learn this valuable lesson and combine the synergy between businesses, real estate, and paper assets. You will find that owning businesses in different industries to be a good idea as well. It behooves you to invest in different types of real estate. You might have some commercial buildings or strip center, some residential single family, duplexes, and some apartment complexes. You need to find what paper assets you are most comfortable with and which ones you seem to understand the best from your education.

Take the time and spend the money to educate yourself on these monetary and investment issues. I can assure you that your financial education, coupled with the lessons that you have learned in this book, will take you further than you expected and sooner than you thought. I know this for a fact because I lived it. I believed.

*Reflections on the Riches from this Chapter*

- If your system goes to sleep at night, then you don't have a system.

- For the investor starting out, it is in your best interest to keep your job and start a business on the side.

- Your goal should be to work yourself out of your job, even if you own the business!

- Leverage your time and money.

- Take the time and spend the money to educate yourself on these monetary and investment issues.

# Chapter 18

# WHAT ARE YOU GOING TO DO TODAY?

Mike Murdock once said, "Winners do daily what losers do occasionally." Develop habits that you do daily. As you create your freedom, you must develop habits that are non-negotiable. There are things that I do on a daily and weekly basis. I don't forget to do them, and I don't skip them. I realize that they are what makes and keeps me on the track of success. I exercise several days a week. I have a time of reflection and meditation each morning. I spend ten minutes to review the business that I want to take care of that day (because it is already written down) and check the balances in my accounts, email, and the status of my stocks and other investments.

I like to take care of phone calls that I need to make first thing because it gives a whole day for events to develop. We're able to accomplish more and it keeps me from having to forward that responsibility on to the next day. That way, I never get behind. I eat right on a daily basis. I don't desire the foods that would cause me to gain weight. Eating right is a daily discipline and habit that I've created in my life. I also wake up around the same time every day. I do not wake up to an alarm clock. I tell my body what time I want to get up the next morning, and I wake up at that time (within one or two minutes) or earlier. I never could do that with an alarm clock.

After my meditation time, exercise, shower, and breakfast, I read a personal development book. I also love to re-read financial literacy books. Because I implemented what I could grasp from the first reading, it prepared me to grasp deeper truths and concepts during the second reading, and I am able to maximize the profits that I receive from a book. When I look at the cost of a book compared to the return I get from it, I count my blessings. If I spend $15 on a book, there are normally several gold nuggets in there that I can use to make several thousand or even several hundred thousand dollars by putting the information from several books together. Action is what gives knowledge its power. I also make sure I eat dinner with my family each night at the dinner table. We eat together and wait for everyone to finish before anyone is allowed to get out of their seat. Even then, we ask to be excused from the table. Good manners should be a habit that you exemplify daily.

You must develop a daily routine—and hitting the snooze button two or three times doesn't count! That's a lousy routine. If you don't exercise, eat right, read, or have a quiet time, then you need to revamp your daily routine because you are doing occasionally what winners do daily. It must become a habit. If you show me what your habits are, I can predict your future. That's right. I can predict what your financial temperature will be five years from now. I can predict what your family relationships will be like. If your daily routine does not include talking (without the TV on) with your spouse or playing with your children, then you will not reap the kind of emotional rewards as those that dedicate time each day to spend with family. It is a great idea to have a family night that you dedicate each week to spending with your family. Do something fun. Go out to eat, and then go bowling. Go fishing on a Saturday. Exercise together. Go on a bike ride. Go to the lake or beach. Play croquet, badminton, volleyball, or "tag" in the front yard. Play hide-and-seek. Play your children in a game of their favorite sport. I can't emphasize to you the importance of doing with them what is important to them.

You will notice in any professional sport or with any professional athlete that their success came at the expense of hard work, much sweat, and an unwavering dedication. It wasn't easy. Their success was grounded in their daily habits–in their routines. Things they did habitually and daily without questioning what they could be doing if they weren't doing that. They closed the back door. They went to the gym at the same time. They exercised consistently. They ate right daily. They trained daily. Your success or failure will be able to be traced to something you did or did not do daily. If you ate doughnuts daily, your obesity and overweight mid-section could be directly linked to your daily habit of eating junk food. If you lose your family, it could be traced back to the lack of time you spent with them on a daily and weekly basis. Oh, I know that you said they were more important to you than anything else, but your daily actions and habits told a different story. To be truly rich and successful, you must develop daily success habits. Eventually, your habits will be performed subconsciously and success will become you and it will feel natural. But you must consciously make it a habit. There are not only daily success habits that you need to form, but there are probably current daily habits that need to be eliminated. I know you really don't want to hear this, but that's what I'm here for. If you wanted a "yes" man, you wouldn't listen to him or respect him, and he certainly wouldn't lead to wealth, success, and happiness, and you know that deep down.

There are daily habits that you need to replace with positive success habits. You might need to end your daily habit of thinking negatively or not thinking positively. You might need to get serious and dedicated about your deteriorating health. You might need to make some good habits about time management. You might need to habitually leave people feeling better about themselves by having been in your presence. Whatever habit you need to start or stop, you must begin immediately, and you must do it daily. No one ever got the top without successfully training themselves daily. A track Olympian doesn't start eating right and running a little bit just one week before tryouts. It is their life. They have disciplined their habits for years to achieve their goal.

All of these suggestions I'm giving to you doesn't cost a thing. Think about it. It is free to change the way you think, yet it will make you tons of money. It is free to stop a habit and to start another one. It doesn't cost a dime to start controlling your mind and belief. These are all things that you can begin right now. In fact, if you aren't sure that you will get the results that I'm talking about, test me. For thirty days, determine that you will control your mind, belief, eating habits, exercise, and family time, and tell me if you aren't on the road to greater prosperity than you've been in the last year. I promise you it works, but the first day that you aren't consistent in these new habits, you must start your thirty days back over again. This plan works. This is the exact method I have used to stay focused toward wealth and riches. It is quite natural now. It is second nature, and it feels like a hobby, not a discipline or habit. This discipline and practice will increase your finances, improve the health of your marriage, and better your health and relationships. You can do it. For the sake of your own success, you must do it. Winners do daily what losers do occasionally. Don't pay half the price. Don't do 90% of the work, but fail to do it consistently. Don't short change yourself and sell yourself short. You are worth it. You deserve to have wealth untold. You deserve to have a loving, nurturing home. You deserve to have the health and happiness that comes from making a difference in the lives of others, being financially free, and having a good home. This is my kind of success, and I wish it for you as well.

*Reflections on the Riches from this Chapter*

- ➣ Develop habits that you do daily.

- ➣ Action is what gives knowledge its power.

- ➣ Good manners should be a daily habit.

- ➣ Your daily habits will predict your future.

- ➣ To be truly rich, you must develop daily success habits.

*Chapter 19*

# CREATE YOUR OWN RUSH

Before you go, there are a couple things I want you to be aware of. This key of the wealthy, successful person will spur and create the action steps that you need to take next. It will continually guide you on your journey. It is a spirit of expectancy. You must develop a spirit of expectancy. Everything you do, every move you make, and every action you take must be taken with a spirit of expectancy and a sense of urgency. By having this spirit of expectancy, it can create a sense of urgency within you. This is mandatory to achieve your goals. A sense of urgency will cause you to take the next step. A sense of urgency will keep you from idleness and pro-crastination. A sense of urgency will not tolerate laziness from you nor from anyone else.

When a person that projects a powerful image has a sense of urgency, things get done. Period! You won't have to wonder if it got done or not. You will know. If you give someone a task to do that has a sense of urgency, you can rest assured that you have placed it in the most capable hands. Likewise, if you are to reach the lofty heights of great riches, you will not be able to do so with a lethargic attitude. There is no half way. It's all the way or no way at all. If you have had disappointed hopes in your life, evaluate the sense of urgency with which you operated and lived. Being committed, dedicated, and persistent just isn't enough. You must have a sense of urgency. That is how deals are made. That is how records are set. That is how quotas are broken. If a salesperson, business owner, or any employee will get a sense of urgency about what they see needs to be done, it will rock their world. They will then be the exception, not the rule. Most people pace themselves in the race of life. They don't give everything 100%. What ends up happening is that they only give 50% to everything. You must give whatever you are doing at that moment 100%. If you are exercising, then do it with all of your heart. Give it your best. If you are playing with your family, give it 100% of your energy and focus. If you are taking care of business, then run hard. Give it all you've got for the allotted amount of time.

I like to call my effort "taking care of business" rather than "working." I do this to help my family know that what I am doing is not to benefit any other company. I am taking care of business to provide the best life that I can for them. I am taking care of business so that I can be the man that I was created to be. When I'm taking care of business, there is a focus, passion, and intensity like you've never seen. I get "in the zone" focused. When you take care of business, what is your spirit like? Do you have a spirit of expectancy and not one of hope? Do you know what results you will get and will accept nothing less? Does that spirit of expectancy develop a sense of urgency in your tone, in your step, and in your eyes? It will show. It will also show if you don't have it. Lacking a sense of urgency will reap you average returns. When people can see the fire in your eyes, that sense of urgency, that eye of the tiger, then you will reap the rewards of the rich and famous. It can be yours, but not by accident. You were born

to live this life. You were born to read this book and be challenged by it. You were born so this book could propel you to
the next book that will take you to the next level. And when
you re-read the timeless truths of this book at a later date,
they will be applicable to where you are during that stage of
your life. Get the eye of the tiger. Live your life with enthusiasm and excitement and never, ever, ever lose your sense of
urgency. It is your first class ticket to achieving your dreams!

*Reflection on the Riches from this Chapter*

- You must give whatever you are doing at the moment 100%

- Call your efforts "taking care of business" rather than "working."

# Chapter 20

# FREEDOM IS THE ONLY THING THAT RINGS

O h, I love this part. I was born to action. My purpose in life is to spur others to action. You must find your venue of influence. Your success will not be fully realized until you make a lasting difference and change for the better in another person's life.

We live in the greatest nation on earth. We aren't without our problems, but we are a great nation. We are a free nation. We enjoy more freedoms than any other country or empire has ever known. But listen to me. Freedom is not free, and it's not for sale. Freedom must be defended. Freedom is expensive. It has been willingly bought with the blood of our loved ones. It has been vigorously defended so that you and I could have the opportunity to live in a free society where we have the freedom to life, liberty, and the pursuit of happiness. We live in a land where we are free to build profitable businesses without the government taking them from us once they reach a certain level of prosperity. We live in a land where we can worship Who, what, when, and where we want to. We live in a land where you are free to be a success or failure, whichever you choose. We live in a land where you, not the government, can decide your fate and what kind of life you live and where you live it. We have so many precious freedoms, but let me tell you something. Don't let our forefathers die in vain. Do something with your life. Make something great of yourself. Don't settle for second best. Don't settle for average or mediocrity. Don't do what you've always done unless you want what you've always gotten. Stand up for what's right, good, decent, and honorable. Don't sit on the sidelines. Don't be a spectator. Get in the game. Be a part of the action. Pursue your dreams with the same intensity that others fought for your freedom. They fought for your national freedom, now it's your turn to fight for your personal freedom and financial freedom.

If for no other reason, you owe it to those who have paid the price for your freedom to go out and be successful in our free enterprise society. Successful people must learn to delay short term gratification for long term security and prosperity. Quitting is not an option. Failure is not an option. Success will prevail. Your goals must be accomplished. There is no turning back. There is no back door. The only way to go out is to go out fighting, believing that your success is around the next corner and in the next investment. And you won't ever let up, give up, or shut up until you're taken up. You must take risks. The biggest risk is not taking a risk at all. You must take educated risks. If you don't get away from the shore, you'll never ride the wave. In fact, you'll start to doubt the wave even exists. I hear broke people talking about the national debt. I'm concerned about where that will lead us in the near future as well, but the national debt isn't what's going to sink America financially—it's the unsecured personal debt that will sink us. That's where the rubber meets the road. Don't get mad at the government for doing the same thing you do every month. You can't change the facts, but you can certainly change the results. You can make a difference, but you must BE the difference. Most Americans are out of shape, out of money, out of hope, and up to their eye balls in debt. And I'm telling you that the answer is for people to get a sense of urgency about life, their finances, their health, and their relationships.

My oldest daughter was born on September 11, 2001 right in-between the two crashes. She was born at 9:00a.m, just two minutes before the second plan crashed into the World Trade Center Tower #2. The instant she was born a nurse burst into the room and turned the TV on just in time for me to turn around and watch that plane fly into the second tower. I was horrified. I thought, "What kind of a world have I just brought my child into? What kind of a world will I be raising her in? What will this change?" I want you to know that things changed a lot in the days that followed. We are just now beginning to figure out the price of freedom, and that you can't wait to be attacked before you start fighting for your freedom. You must be in the "fighting mode" long before your freedom is attacked. When your personal financial situation comes under attack, Friend, it's too late to start fighting for your freedom. It's already been infringed upon. The time to start fighting for your family and your freedom is now. Don't accept the slavery of a boss or a job. Don't let someone tell you when to take vacation and how long you can be gone. Don't let your manager decide how much money you make, how much house you can afford, what kind of car you can drive, and what kind of vacations you can take. Take your freedom back. Stand up and fight for your freedom. Start a business. Build a business. Invest in real estate. Learn how to make money with paper assets. Invest in your financial education and raise your financial I.Q. That is how you fight for your financial freedom. That is how you fight for your personal freedom. You can't look back. You can't afford to criticize yourself and the lack thus far in your life with negative self-talk. You must be on the vigilant offensive. You cannot accept defeat. You must learn from your mistakes and turn your failures into the stepping stones of success. You can be great. You can achieve everything you've ever desired, but you must pay the price. You won't find the price on sale. You won't find it at the discount store. You will only find the kind of freedom and success you desire on the shelves of hard work, persistence, constant enthusiasm, financial literacy, and the backbone and courage necessary to fight the nay-sayers on your way to the top. Everybody has them—those who say you can't do it, that you will never make it. One of you will be right. Those who want to be successful will find a way. Those who don't will find an excuse.

Thank you for reading this book. I wish you all the success you believe in.

### *My Story*

I was born in Birmingham, Alabama. Our family moved to Florida when I was five years old. We lived there for four years while my dad went to college. He graduated with a Biblical Studies major and became a pastor in West Virginia as well as the Administrator of their Christian academy. My mother has her bachelor's degree in Secondary Education and has taught in that school from that day until now. Upon my high school graduation, I moved to Knoxville, Tennessee to go to college. I got my Bachelor's degree in five semesters. It was a major accomplishment for me. However, that is not the only thing I achieved during this short time frame. My parents were not able to provide much financial support for my college bills, and I did not want to get student loans. I worked a full time job during my college years. I worked from 3pm until midnight Monday through Friday. On Saturday and Sunday, I worked as an intern an hour and a half away from the college. When I was nineteen (between my first and second years of college), I bought my first house. I bought my first investment house within seven months, and in less than eight months time, or my graduation date, I walked across that stage and received my diploma with a net worth of $700,000. My goal was to be worth one million dollars. I fell short, but I was not too disappointed with all of my accomplishments. I would reach one million in net worth within four months of graduation. I got cocky and content with what I had. I bought a great SUV, a convertible, and a lake house. I started letting my past successes keep me from taking care of business. My lack of focus and attention to my real estate proved disastrous. My agent had made some significant mistakes with our financing and cash flow, and I got a bill one day in the mail from a construction loan that I had that was due in a week in the amount of $247,000. I didn't leave this kind of cash sitting around, and I didn't have that kind of liquid capital available anywhere. I was already over-leveraged. I explored several options for a couple of months with a headstrong intensity. This circumstance jolted me back to reality and jerked me down off of my high horse. I was back into the reality that my past decision making had created for me.

Those were some of the darkest days that I would go through. I remember my Dad saying, "Well, you were worth more than most people will ever be worth, and you are poorer than most people will ever be." He was right. I had been on both extremes, and I was going through the worst financial nightmare anyone can imagine. I remember trying to find

15–20 cents to go to the grocery store to buy ramen noodles only to realize that I didn't have enough gas in the car to make it to the grocery store a mile away. I remember putting 30 cents into the gas tank to go to the grocery store and buying 25 cents worth of groceries. It was the most humbling time of my life. It's hard for an empty bag to stand up straight, and I had the wind knocked out of me. I remember sitting out by the lake and thinking to myself, "This is the poorest I will ever be the rest of my life." I determined in those dark days that I would never again lose sight of my business. I would never rest on my laurels and think that I had arrived. I committed to myself that I was a winner and that whatever it took, I would rebuild my financial empire, and I would be richer than I ever had hoped to be.

My wife, newborn daughter, and I moved from our lake house to a 900 square foot apartment. Nine months later, we moved into a home that was worth more than twice the amount of our lake house. I had paid off all of our debt. We were back on track. Nothing was going to keep us down! Everyone gets knocked down, but it takes a winner to get back up and keep going. We moved into our brand new 5 bedroom, 4 bath home with 20 foot high ceilings in the living room, and a 14 foot high, brick-arched fireplace. It was a home beyond our comprehension. We refused to lose focus that time. Within 13 months from the day we bought that home, we bought another quarter million dollar investment property that we bought with $110,000 worth of equity in it. I began to diversify my income into different asset classes, and the synergy of money began to grow my money exponentially.

One of the reasons I wrote this book is because I've had money, and I've been broke, and rich is certainly better! I love it when I hear that a true millionaire could do it all over again and probably quicker because of his financial education and the lessons that he learned. I have learned what not to do. I know how to get wealthy when you have money and when you have less than nothing. No matter what your current financial situation, you can be rich. You might have to be more creative the more difficult your situation, but it is possible. The worse things got, the more creative I had to be. That creativity has served me well. I remember sitting at a real estate seminar one day and the instructor was talking about the different ways a specific deal could be structured. A couple of suggestions were given, and the instructor said that it would be impossible and had never happened before. I grinned because I had done several of those things that they felt were impossible. They believed too heavily in market conditions and statistics and did not have a creative investment eye. They only knew the traditional investment strategy. My situation wasn't traditional so I learned what I could do if I had to. That education has been invaluable to me. A rich person could lose everything today and within a short period of time, be wealthier than they ever were before.

I would love to speak at your next seminar or success conference. I also speak in high schools, colleges, churches, individual athletes or athletic teams prior to games. If you would like to schedule me, please contact me using the information below. My presentation is a dynamic blend of the things I talk about in this book. The results I have helped others attain are real and tangible. Thank you for giving me the opportunity to serve you and increase your wealth.

ROLLAN ROBERTS

info@rollanroberts.com

www.rollanroberts.com